P9-DMI-818

ENDPAPER

Dauntless dive bombers from the United States aircraft carrier *Enterprise* head for safety after setting off a fatal conflagration on the flight deck of the Japanese flattop *Akagi.* The action, painted for The Epic of Flight by the eminent aviation artist R. G. Smith, took place on June 4, 1942, at the Battle of Midway, a pivotal U.S. victory in the Pacific during World War II.

THE CARRIER WAR

Other Publications:

FIX IT YOURSELF
FITNESS, HEALTH AND NUTRITION
SUCCESSFUL PARENTING
HEALTHY HOME COOKING
UNDERSTANDING COMPUTERS
LIBRARY OF NATIONS
THE ENCHANTED WORLD
THE KODAK LIBRARY OF CREATIVE PHOTOGRAPHY
GREAT MEALS IN MINUTES
THE CIVIL WAR
PLANET EARTH
COLLECTOR'S LIBRARY OF THE CIVIL WAR
THE GOOD COOK
WORLD WAR II
HOME REPAIR AND IMPROVEMENT
THE OLD WEST

For information on and a full description of any of the Time-Life Books series listed above, please write:

Reader Information
Time-Life Books
541 North Fairbanks Court
Chicago, Illinois 60611

This volume is one of a series that traces the adventure and science of aviation, from the earliest manned balloon ascension through the era of jet flight.

THE CARRIER WAR

by Clark G. Reynolds

AND THE EDITORS OF TIME-LIFE BOOKS

TIME-LIFE BOOKS, ALEXANDRIA, VIRGINIA

THE AUTHOR

Clark G. Reynolds, curator of the museum aircraft carrier U.S.S. *Yorktown* at Patriots Point, South Carolina, has taught at the U.S. Naval Academy at Annapolis. He is the author of *The Fast Carriers: The Forging of an Air Navy* and has written numerous articles on military history.

THE CONSULTANT for The Carrier War

E. T. Wooldridge Jr. is the Curator for Aeronautics at the National Air and Space Museum in Washington, D.C., and author of *The P-80 Shooting Star: Evolution of a Jet Fighter.* A graduate of the U.S. Naval Academy at Annapolis, he has cruised the Atlantic and the Mediterranean as a fighter pilot aboard various aircraft carriers, including the U.S.S. *Independence* and the U.S.S. *Enterprise.*

THE CONSULTANTS for The Epic of Flight

Charles Harvard Gibbs-Smith was Research Fellow at the Science Museum, London, and a Keeper-Emeritus of the Victoria and Albert Museum, London. He wrote or edited some 20 books and numerous articles on aeronautical history. In 1978 he was the first Lindbergh Professor of Aerospace History at the National Air and Space Museum, Smithsonian Institution, Washington.

Dr. Hidemasa Kimura, honorary professor at Nippon University, Tokyo, is the author of numerous books on the history of aviation and is a widely known authority on aeronautical engineering and aircraft design. One plane that he designed established a world distance record in 1938.

Fourth printing. Revised 1987.
Printed in U.S.A.
Published simultaneously in Canada.
School and library distribution by Silver Burdett Company, Morristown, New Jersey.

Library of Congress Cataloguing in Publication Data
Reynolds, Clark G.
The carrier war.
(The Epic of flight)
Bibliography: p.
Includes index.
1. World War, 1939-1945 — Aerial operations. 2. World War, 1939-1945 — Naval operations. 3. World War, 1939-1945 — Pacific Ocean. 4. Aircraft carriers — History. 5. Naval aviation — History. I. Time-Life Books. II. Series.
D785.R4 940.54'49 81-18209
ISBN 0-8094-3304-4 AACR2
ISBN 0-8094-3305-3 (lib. bdg.)
ISBN 0-8094-3306-0 (deluxe)
ISBN 0-8094-3307-9 (retail ed.)

CONTENTS

1	**Wings for the world's navies**	**21**
2	**Blunting the Japanese onslaught**	**61**
3	**Turning point at Midway**	**83**
4	**Collisions on the road to Tokyo**	**115**
5	**"We wish for the best place after death"**	**151**
	Acknowledgments	172
	Picture credits	172
	Bibliography	173
	Index	174

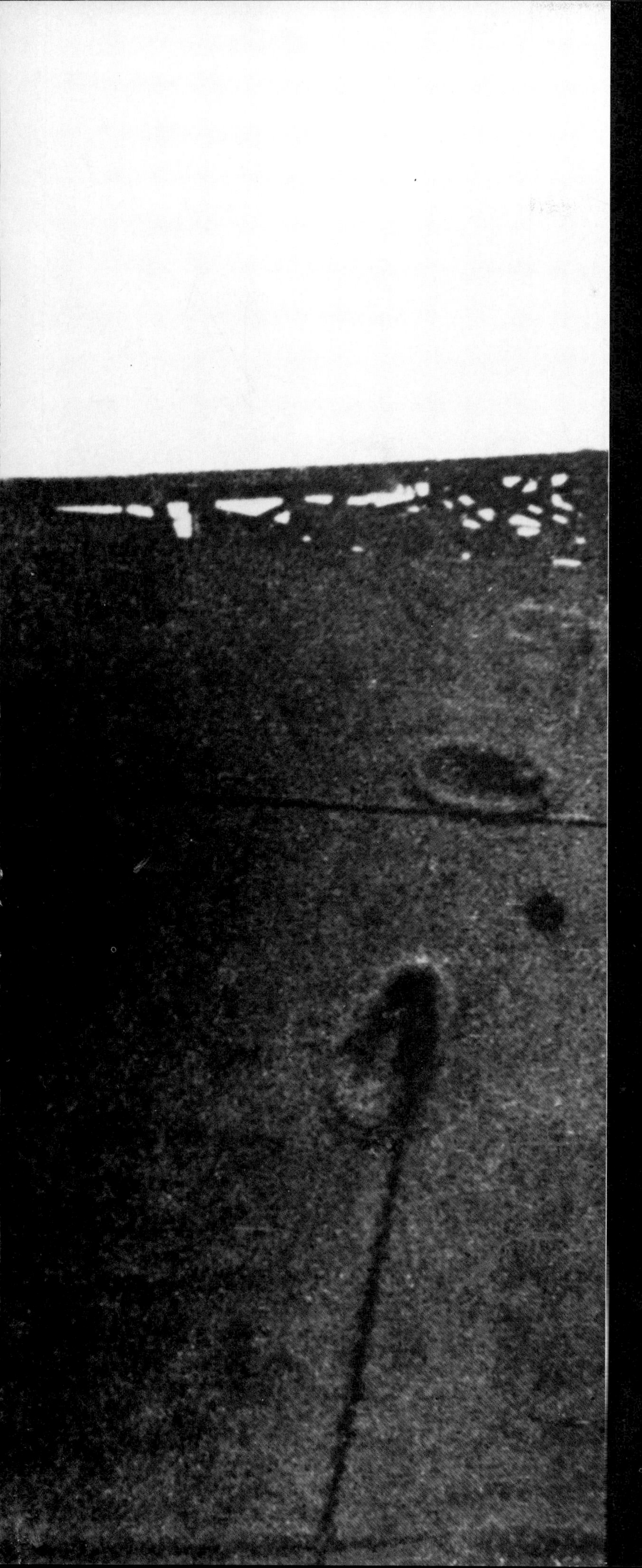

Genesis of the carrier

The realization that the airplane could play a part in naval warfare appears to have struck three naval officers—one each from the British, American and French fleets—at the same time and in the same place. The improbable scene was an inland plain near the French city of Rheims, where in August 1909 the three were official observers at an international air show. There they saw aircraft perform previously unheard-of feats: flying 112 nonstop miles, attaining altitudes of 500 feet and blazing along at 47 miles an hour.

Such heady performances inspired the three attachés to advise their superiors that the airplane might one day provide far-seeing eyes for a fleet or even become an offensive weapon. Before this could happen, however, a way would have to be found to get the frail, short-range aircraft aloft at sea.

The first such attempt took place in the United States in late 1910, when a young barnstorming pilot named Eugene Ely flew a plane from a ramp built on the deck of a United States Navy cruiser. Two months later, in another experimental flight, he landed his aircraft on another naval vessel, a feat made possible by an ingenious arresting gear—ropes stretched between sandbags—that slowed and stopped the plane.

Ely's epochal flights had shown that ships could be used as floating airfields, but the development of effective aircraft carriers would be a long process marked by painful trial and error. During World War I, the British Royal Navy took the lead, experimenting initially with seaplanes and then with warships bearing wooden ramps from which landplanes could take off—and on which they sometimes managed to land. Only after the War's end, however, did Britain—and the United States and Japan—produce true aircraft carriers with flight decks on which planes could routinely land as well as take off. These would be the prototypes of the hulking, complex flattops that revolutionized naval warfare in World War II and proved to be the most powerful seagoing weapons in history.

Making his pioneering takeoff, stunt pilot Eugene Ely coaxes his Curtiss biplane from the U.S.S. Birmingham's makeshift flight deck and mushes downward toward the waters of Hampton Roads, Virginia. The plane actually brushed the water before Ely gained altitude and flew two and a half miles to land near the Norfolk naval base.

watch from every vantage point, Eugene Ely swoops in from a flight over San Francisco Bay for the first landing of a plane on a ship.

In the photographs at right, Ely's Curtiss nears the ramp, picks up the crude rope-and-sandbag arresting gear and stops safely near the Pennsylvania's superstructure.

Sailors stand on the edge of a sloping takeoff ramp on the bow of the camouflage-striped Pegasus, a World War I British carrier. The vessel could launch its four or five Sopwith Pup landplanes from the ramp. Its four seaplanes were housed in hangars aft and lowered into the sea for takeoff.

Crewmen ease a pontoon-equipped biplane into a seaplane carrier's hangar in 1915.

Takeoff ramps for seaplane tenders

World War I brought a flurry of activity in seagoing aviation as the British Royal Navy searched for ways of deploying bombers and scouting planes against the German enemy.

At first, aircraft with pontoons, known then as hydroaeroplanes, seemed to be most suitable for duty with the fleet; they could operate from what one enthusiast called the "universal airdrome"—the water. In 1914 the British Admiralty commandeered a half-dozen large, fast ferryboats and converted them into seaplane carriers. But nature's watery airfield was usually far too turbulent for the floatplanes to take off from, and those that did manage to get aloft were slow and clumsy in the air.

After a series of foul-weather fiascoes with seaplanes, the Royal Navy decided to try more agile landplanes. In November 1915 a young Navy lieutenant, B. F. Fowler, flew his fighter from a moving warship. Fowler knew, however, that he would not be able to return to his ship, the seaplane carrier H.M.S. *Vindex*. Its rudimentary flight deck was not long enough for a landing, so the pilot ditched his plane in the sea.

Lieutenant Fowler's Bristol Scout is prepared for its takeoff from the H.M.S. Vindex.

The Furious prepares to retrieve a seaplane (lower right) from the water. Designed as a slim-hulled cruiser, the ship had very narrow flight decks.

During an early test, a skid-equipped Sopwith Pup careens down the Furious' deck, dragging a wing tip before halting (right) near the final barrier of vertical cables.

A crane lifts a Sopwith fighter through a wide hatchway from the Furious' hold, which was a precursor of the cavernous hangar decks of later aircraft carriers.

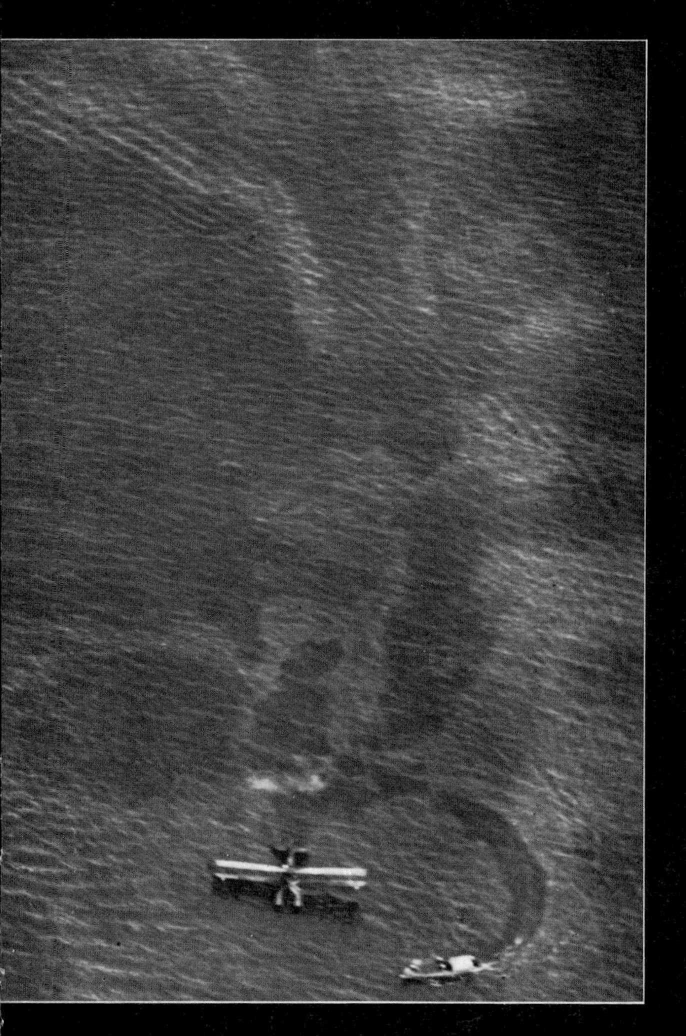

A "monstrosity" with two flight decks

A vessel that could launch planes but on which they could not land was only half a floating airfield, so late in World War I the British tried to complete the carrier's development with a conversion of the cruiser *Furious*. The result, said one historian, was "an aircraft carrier at both ends and a monstrosity amidships."

The ship's superstructure divided the flight deck in two. Worse, hot gases from the funnel and air eddies swirling past the bridge created such turbulence over the afterdeck that landing was almost suicidal. Wires strung along the deck to guide and slow incoming planes proved nearly useless. When the ship went into service in 1918, no landings were allowed.

The success of the floating flatiron

The British learned from the *Furious'* horrible example. In 1918 they fitted a half-built ocean liner's hull with a flight deck that ran the length of the ship. The resulting vessel was christened the *Argus*, but Royal Navy seamen called her the Flat Iron. Despite her featureless, ponderous look, the *Argus* turned out to be the first effective carrier ever built.

The British achieved a flatiron profile by placing the chartroom, from which the *Argus* was conned, on an elevator that lowered it beneath the flight deck during air operations. The rest of the bridge was tucked below the flight deck near the bow and the funnel was eliminated by channeling engine exhausts through pipes to the stern.

Completed too late for World War I, the *Argus* was used for valuable experiments in the 1920s. In one trial, the Admiralty put a bogus "island" superstructure on one side of the deck *(below)* to see if it interfered with aircraft. It did not, and such islands, centralizing control of a ship's operations, became standard features on future carriers.

A Sopwith fighter makes the first landing on the Argus in October 1918. The arresting gear, which proved a failure, used hooks on the planes' landing gear that engaged fore-and-aft guide wires while raised wooden slats bumped the aircraft to a halt.

The Argus sprouts fake funnels and a bridge during tests of an abovedeck control center.

A Blackburn reconnaissance plane lands on the Argus' flat deck in 1928. The masts projecting from the flight deck held radio antennas.

Various aircraft on the Argus' hangar deck include a fighter with wings that folded to fit the elevator (left).

The Langley shows her latticework sides as a Vought fighter settles toward the flight deck.

The tail hook of a Vought scout plane grabs an arresting cable as the aircraft touches down on the U.S.S. Langley in 1930. The auxiliary fore-and-aft cables strung on supports were later discarded.

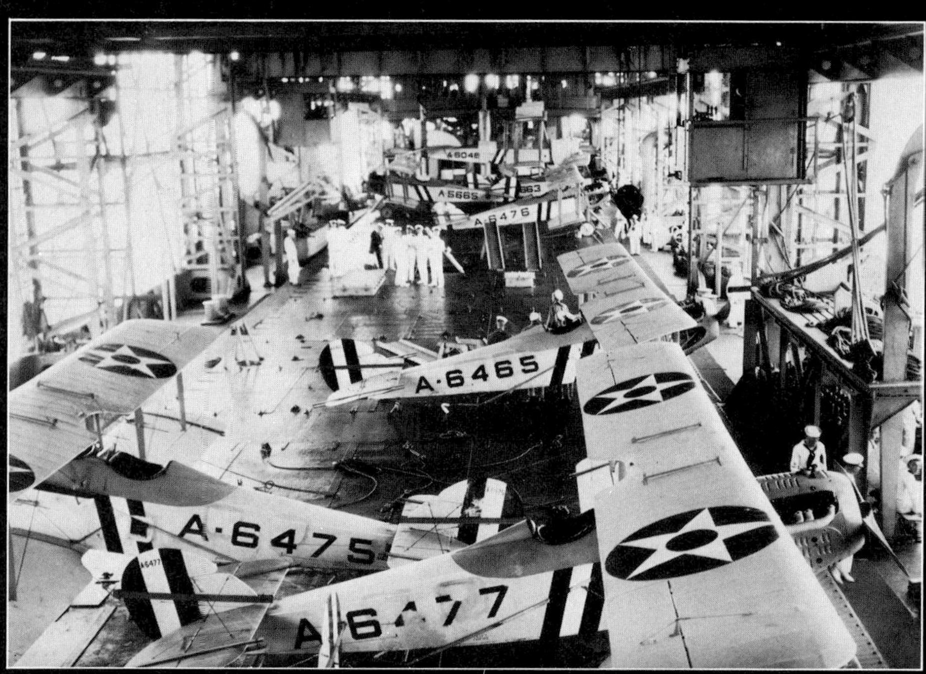

A welding shop and other repair facilities (right) line one side of the Langley's hangar deck. Boards were fastened to the planes' tail surfaces to keep them from flapping while the aircraft were in storage.

A roughhewn American pioneer

The U.S. Navy's first flattop, the *Langley*, quickly earned an apt nickname: the Covered Wagon. Built on a collier's hull, the vessel was high-sided, blunt-ended, and with a top speed of 14 knots, moved with the heavy dignity of a prairie schooner. The ungainly ship's hangar deck was open to weather on the sides and her twin smokestacks hung awkwardly over the side during air operations.

Yet the *Langley*, which was commissioned in 1922, was an invaluable floating laboratory for carrier design and operations. Her hangar deck had extensive repair facilities, making her an almost self-sufficient floating airfield. Most important, her arresting gear—tail hooks on the planes engaged cables strung laterally across the flight deck and attached to a braking system—worked so well that it would become standard equipment on the carriers of every nation.

Its short funnels belching smoke, Japan's first aircraft carrier, the Hosho, steams off the Japanese coast during sea trials in 1922.

The first generation of purebred flattops

After nearly a decade of experiments in making seagoing airfields of cruisers, coal ships and ocean liners, the first carriers to be built as such from the keel up appeared in the 1920s. First finished, in 1922, was Japan's *Hosho (above).* The name meant "Swooping Dragon," but the tiny 7,500-ton ship was hardly ferocious. Nonetheless, it was the keystone of the mighty Japanese carrier fleet that would range the Pacific in 1941.

The next from-the-keel-up carrier was Britain's *Hermes (left),* commissioned in 1924. The United States was last to build such a carrier, launching the 14,500-ton *Ranger (opposite)* in 1933.

Britain's Hermes appears unbalanced by its tall island. With few antiaircraft guns and only 12 planes, the small carrier would be easily sunk by Japanese bombers in 1942.

The U.S.S. Ranger's flight deck bristles with more than 50 planes during a prewar cruise in the Atlantic in 1941. Although smaller than most major U.S. carriers of the era, the ship could handle up to 72 aircraft.

1
Wings for the world's navies

In 1910, stunt pilot Eugene B. Ely relished the notion of flying an airplane off a ship, but he got a good many arguments against doing so. Wilbur Wright, one of the foremost aviation experts of the era, said that such an attempt would be too dangerous. Ely's own employer, Glenn Curtiss—an archrival of Wright's and the man who built the plane that Ely wanted to fly—tried to discourage him. The Secretary of the United States Navy refused money to finance the experiment, and critics of the idea noted that Ely could not even swim.

But he remained determined. Exuding the supreme self-confidence that typified the coterie of civilian daredevil pilots of which he was a member, and encouraged by Captain Washington I. Chambers, the Navy's first director of aviation, Ely succeeded in gaining the use of the scout cruiser *Birmingham* in Hampton Roads, Virginia. Private funds provided by an aviation enthusiast paid for the construction of an 83-foot-long ramp that sloped downward toward the sea over the ship's forecastle, and the Navy set aside November 14 for the experiment. Ely would fly one of Curtiss' pushers that had been pieced together from two wrecked ones.

The plane's engine did not arrive until the appointed morning, but Ely and his mechanics aboard the ship managed to install it in time. Then the *Birmingham* took such an agonizingly long time to weigh anchor that an approaching autumn squall threatened to dash the whole scheme. Seeing his opportunity about to escape him, the anxious Ely revved up his engine before the ship was under way, signaled for his plane to be released and rolled down the ramp toward the bow—and the water. Sailors and guests gasped as the pusher dropped over the bow and fought for altitude. Salt spray fogged Ely's goggles and the water lapped up at his wheels. But he kept his craft aloft, headed for shore and set down on the nearest beach.

Although the world's press was electrified, Navy officials were not. The ramp had made some of the ship's guns inoperable, they harrumphed, adding that the flight had been a mere stunt. But Ely was

Proving the usefulness of ships as floating airfields, resolute Eugene Ely—sporting a football helmet, goggles and a safety harness rigged from an inner tube—prepares to lift off from the cruiser U.S.S. Pennsylvania in 1911, soon after making the first shipboard landing.

unfazed and told Captain Chambers that he now wanted to try the more difficult feat of landing on a ship.

Impressed by Ely's resolve, Chambers pulled more strings and arranged to have an even longer platform mounted over the stern of the cruiser *Pennsylvania,* based in San Francisco Bay. To stop the plane, 22 ropes—each fastened to a 50-pound sandbag at each end—were stretched taut across the ramp at three-foot intervals. Ely had fitted hooks on his half-ton Curtiss pusher to engage the lines as the plane touched down; the weight of the bags would then drag the craft to a halt.

Just before 11 a.m. on January 18, 1911, Ely took off from the local Army airfield, flew toward the anchored *Pennsylvania,* cut his throttle 50 feet from the ramp and set his plane down. The hooks snagged the last 12 lines, and the plane stopped in some 30 feet. Cheering onlookers were outdone in their enthusiasm by the captain of the cruiser, who announced that the event was "the most important landing of a bird since the dove flew back to the ark." Then he ordered the plane positioned for takeoff over the stern. After lunch with the captain, Ely roared down the 120-foot ramp, executed the second takeoff of an airplane from a ship and landed safely back at the Army base.

The San Francisco Examiner had no doubts about Ely's achievement. "Eugene Ely Revises World's Naval Tactics," the newspaper proclaimed the next day. Indeed, in one stroke, Ely had demonstrated the feasibility of what in time would become the most powerful weapon that a navy could possess: an aircraft carrier, a ship capable of transporting warplanes to battle anywhere in the world, launching them against an enemy and retrieving them to strike again and again.

But these revolutionary men-of-war would mature slowly. The mere idea of such ships raised the hackles of traditionalist admirals, and the trenches of World War I would be plowed under before the first true aircraft carriers were ready to go into action. But by the outbreak of World War II, after more than two decades of experiment and development, these magnificent ships would be poised to alter irrevocably the complexion of naval warfare. In the Pacific, where two of the world's most powerful carrier navies stood opposed, mighty battleships—built to hammer at one another with huge guns—rarely played a decisive role. Instead they fended off diving aircraft that dropped bombs, launched torpedoes and raked decks with cannon and machine-gun fire. Without carriers of its own, a battleship navy was powerless to retaliate against the nests from which these angry hornets swarmed.

From the Coral Sea to Midway and back across the Pacific to the very threshhold of Japan, flattops supplanted battlewagons as the capital ships to be reckoned with. In other theaters of operation around the world as well as in the Pacific, carriers softened beachheads for amphibious assault, escorted troop and supply convoys safely across hostile waters and, working with clutches of destroyers, made submarining one of the most hazardous and least rewarding duties in enemy navies. But it was in the Pacific, where Japanese flattops met those of the United

An irrepressible British innovator

The man who led Britain into the forefront of aircraft carrier development was Lieutenant Charles Rumney Samson, a roughhewn adventurer who was praised by his superiors as capable of "carrying out any new work with success."

In January 1912 Samson became the second man ever to take off from a ship, flying a Short S.38 biplane from a platform erected on the battleship *Africa.* That same year, he made the first takeoff from a moving ship, demonstrating to the Admiralty that carriers could launch planes into battle without stopping and thus becoming easy targets for enemy submarines or aircraft.

Samson was also the first person to fly a folding-wing aircraft, an innovation that would solve storage problems on carriers of the future. And he was the first commander of the naval wing of the Royal Flying Corps—itself the world's first carrier-based air force.

Samson inspects a folding-wing seaplane.

Sailors load Samson's Short S.38 aboard a coal barge for the trip to the H.M.S. Africa, which lay at anchor in Sheerness harbor.

Parked on a platform above the Africa's forecastle (above), Samson prepares for takeoff. Four months later, on the Hibernia (right), he proved that a moving runway was no obstacle to successful takeoff.

States in battles contested on a grander scale than any previous naval engagements in history, that the real Carrier War was fought.

Ely foresaw the importance of the aircraft carrier, in principle if not in detail. A week after his aerial visit to the *Pennsylvania,* he wrote to Captain Chambers of his flight: "I have proved that a machine can leave a ship and return to it, and others have proved that an aeroplane can remain in the air for a long time." Ely concluded that the value of "the aeroplane for the Navy is unquestioned." But, except for a few far-sighted men like Chambers, the United States Navy did not share Ely's view. An entire decade and a world war would pass before another plane would land aboard an American naval vessel, and the development of the aircraft carrier would be left to the British.

Erect and watchful, Sir David Beatty wears the uniform of a vice admiral in this picture taken early in World War I. Later, as the commander of the British Grand Fleet, he was a strong advocate of shipborne planes, saying, "in the future no fleet will be fully equipped for war without aircraft."

"There seems to be something wrong with our bloody ships today," muttered Vice Admiral Sir David Beatty, commander of the Royal Navy's Battle Cruiser Fleet, to his chief of staff. It was a supreme understatement. His prize 27,000-ton battle cruiser *Queen Mary* had just exploded and sunk beneath the North Sea, the victim of well-placed salvos from German warships. Not half an hour earlier, the same end had come to the 18,750-ton cruiser *Indefatigable.* It was the late afternoon of May 31, 1916, and the opening phase of the Battle of Jutland, the one epic (though indecisive) naval engagement of World War I, had already claimed two of Britain's newest and proudest ships.

The battle cruiser, designed by the British as a wide-ranging scout for the fleet, was lightly armored so that it could speed away from enemy guns, carrying vital information for the battleships of the main force. This sacrifice of armor now proved fatal. In the shell flashes that instantaneously detonated the *Queen Mary* and the *Indefatigable,* the battle cruiser was shown to be a failure as the eyes of the fleet.

Only minutes before the calamity, however, a new British scout had appeared on the scene—a pontoon-equipped Short Sunbeam seaplane. Hoisted over the stern of the seaplane carrier *Engadine*—a converted, unarmed cross-Channel packet—the aircraft had taken off with Flight Lieutenant Frederick J. Rutland of the Royal Naval Air Service at the controls. An assistant paymaster from the ship sat in the rear seat as observer. Low clouds forced Rutland—inevitably known thereafter as Rutland of Jutland—to fly below 900 feet and restricted his view to some two or three miles. The guns of four German light cruisers tried their best to shoot him down but he still managed to radio three sighting reports of enemy ships to the *Engadine*—the first time that an airplane had tapped out a wireless message to a fleet in battle.

Although the plane's fuel line broke just before the two fleets clashed, forcing Rutland to glide powerless toward the *Engadine,* his performance had demonstrated to Admiral Beatty the value of ship-based reconnaissance aircraft in battle. But seaplanes were not the ideal craft for the fleet. They could take off and land only in relatively calm waters, uncommon in the North Sea. Moreover, their pontoons made them so

Flight Lieutenant Frederick J. Rutland, who became the first pilot to take part in a naval engagement—the Battle of Jutland, in 1916—relaxes aboard the seaplane carrier H.M.S. Engadine. Rutland was awarded the Distinguished Service Cross for scouting German warships on his historic flight.

sluggish that they could not climb fast enough to overtake and shoot down German Zeppelins, the shore-based eyes of the enemy fleet. Wheeled aircraft were the obvious answer: With their greater speed and higher rate of climb, they could challenge the Zeppelins and perform reconnaissance duties with equal facility. Such planes also had an obvious drawback. They would have to operate from ships, and the Royal Navy had not yet built a vessel that could handle them.

Naval officers had, however, been working on a solution. Less than 14 months after Ely's trailblazing takeoff from the cruiser *Birmingham,* Lieutenant Charles R. Samson of the Royal Navy had repeated the stunt from a platform built over the bow of the battleship *Africa (page 23).* But it took the urgency of World War I and the threat of the Zeppelins to spur the Royal Navy to further action.

Early in 1916, a few months before Rutland's flight, the Navy conducted experiments on the Isle of Grain in the Thames estuary near London. Wheeled planes were successfully landed on a 200-foot platform built roughly the width of a cruiser. At the same time, Captain Murray Sueter, the first Director of the Admiralty's Air Department, sponsored a design by Lieutenant Commander Gerard Homes, a naval architect, for a ship on which pilots could not only take off but land. With modifications the design was accepted, and in August the Admiralty purchased an unfinished ocean liner that a British shipyard had been building for Italy. The ship would be finished as the *Argus,* a 21-knot vessel with a 470-foot flush deck intended for launching and recovering wheeled fighters and reconnaissance aircraft.

But the *Argus* would take at least 14 months to complete. In the meantime, the Royal Navy would have to make do with improvised carriers that would prove only partially satisfactory. The first of these compromises was a series of seaplane carriers, some of them fitted with a takeoff platform built over the bow, much like Samson's platform on the *Africa.* Such a ship, the seaplane carrier *Campania,* was part of the Grand Fleet at the time of the Battle of Jutland. The ship had a 200-foot platform from which seaplanes could go aloft—their pontoons resting on wheeled trolleys that were left behind at takeoff—but returning planes had to land on the water alongside the vessel and then be hoisted aboard. The *Campania,* however, was not present at the battle; she had ingloriously missed the order to sail against the German fleet, leaving the show to the less sophisticated *Engadine*—which had no flight deck—and the glory to Frederick Rutland.

Toward the end of 1916, Rutland was assigned as senior aviator to the *Manxman,* a Channel packet just completing conversion to a seaplane carrier. Plans for the *Manxman* had not included a takeoff platform; Admiral Beatty thought such platforms unnecessary for use with seaplanes. But Rutland argued that a takeoff platform would allow the *Manxman* to launch landplanes as well. True, most of them would be lost after one flight, because they would have to come down in the sea. But many seaplanes were lost under the same circumstances and it was

In an early experiment staged off the British coast, a Sopwith two-seater flies from a platform built on a gun turret of the battle cruiser Australia.

A Sopwith Camel rises from the surface of its seagoing airfield—a flat-decked barge being towed through the North Sea by a destroyer.

clear the sluggish seaplanes could not neutralize the German Zeppelins.

Beatty relented, and a 60-foot platform was built on the *Manxman's* bow. Rutland had a Sopwith Pup fighter barged to the ship. Then, with Beatty aboard, the *Manxman* headed into the Firth of Forth. Rutland climbed into the Pup, and the ship turned into the wind. No one was prepared for how quickly the plane became airborne: When Rutland pushed the throttle forward, the Pup took off in less than 15 feet. It "went up so fast," Ernest Watson, an engineering officer on the *Manxman,* wrote years later, "it looked as though a giant had kicked it up."

Two British fliers clamber aboard a battleship after bringing their plane down in a choppy sea. Until aircraft carriers were fitted with landing decks, returning pilots had no choice but to plunge their planes into the water alongside the ship.

Perhaps more remarkable than Rutland's spectacular takeoff was his success in convincing his pilots that they were better off splashing down in a Pup or similar aircraft than in a seaplane. To prove his point, Rutland had a pilot land a seaplane in a heavy chop on the Firth of Forth. Soon after the engine stopped, the tail of the wave-tossed aircraft dipped into the water, and before long the plane sank. Similar tests had proved that wheeled aircraft, lighter than the seaplanes, would float almost indefinitely if fitted with flotation bags in the fuselage.

Rutland's success in taking off from the *Manxman* led to a suggestion for a more versatile means than specially designed seaplane carriers for taking Navy aircraft to battle—placing the planes aboard the warships themselves. The proposal met considerable resistance. Not only would a takeoff platform on the bow obstruct a ship's forward gun turret, but the ship would have to turn into the wind to launch its plane. Such diversions in battle were thought intolerable. However, since Rutland had shown that the platform could theoretically be as short as 15 feet, a compromise was reached. Fighters were assigned to light cruisers, but not to the mighty battleships; their guns were sacrosanct.

The *Yarmouth* was the first cruiser fitted with what the Royal Navy called a flying-off platform. In August 1917, she joined a light-cruiser squadron covering a mine-laying operation off Denmark. Just after dawn on August 21, lookouts spotted Zeppelin *L 23* shadowing the ships from a distance of about 12 miles. When the squadron turned toward the open sea, the Zeppelin followed. Then Flight Sublieutenant B. A. Smart climbed into his Sopwith Pup and took off; in 10 minutes he had gained enough altitude to attack the Zeppelin from above. He dived on the hydrogen-filled airship, his Lewis gun cracking sharply above the roar of his engine. But if his bullets hit the Zeppelin, they did so without apparent effect, so he climbed and attacked again. This time the airship burst into flame and sagged toward the sea. Smart then set his Sopwith gently on the water and was rescued by a British destroyer.

Several weeks after Smart's feat, Rutland demonstrated to the admirals how they could equip battleships with aircraft without obstructing the ships' guns or, in many instances, forcing the vessels to turn into the wind. A flying-off deck was simply mounted on top of the guns; the turret could then be turned to point the aircraft into the wind for takeoff allowing the ship to maintain its course. But fighting ships with takeoff platforms grafted onto them could carry only one or two aircraft, too few for sustained operations. To solve this problem, yet another—and by far the grandest—interim solution to the aircraft-carrier problem appeared. It was the *Furious.* On this 30-knot cruiser, the Royal Navy constructed a 228-foot-long takeoff deck in place of the forward turret. On a spacious hangar deck below this platform, the *Furious* could carry six Sopwith Pups and four Short seaplanes.

The *Furious* joined the fleet in July 1917, and air operations under the ship's senior flying officer, Squadron Commander E. H. Dunning, proceeded normally: The planes took off from the deck and landed in the sea, where they were often lost. Dunning persuaded the ship's captain to let him try landing on the platform. It would be risky. To produce enough head wind for a landing on the short platform, the *Furious* would have to be under way. Dunning would have to approach from the direction of the stern and then slip in front of the ship's bridge. He made his first two landings easily, but on the third, his plane had mechanical problems and lurched overboard; Dunning was drowned.

Fred Rutland, who had been experimenting with the takeoff platform aboard the *Yarmouth,* replaced Dunning on the *Furious* and argued that the ship's superstructure should be replaced with a flush deck like the one that would be built on the *Argus.* The Admiralty compromised by ordering the *Furious* back into the yards in November 1917 to have her 18-inch gun aft replaced with a 284-foot landing deck. When she rejoined the fleet the following March, the *Furious* immediately undertook landing trials, but with nearly disastrous results. Gases from the smokestack created turbulence over the stern, and the kitelike fighters succeeded in only three out of 13 landings. Even Rutland went over the side and narrowly escaped drowning. Luckily, there were no fatalities, but plans for further landings were abandoned.

In the *Furious,* the British had half an aircraft carrier, a speedy ship that could launch aircraft but could not safely take them aboard after a mission. Even so, the Navy dispatched this fledgling carrier on a daring sneak attack against a Zeppelin base at Tondern in northern Germany. For this mission, the Pup fighters were replaced by far superior machines—Sopwith Camels. At dawn on July 19, 1918, seven Camels—each bearing two 50-pound bombs—took off from the *Furious* and headed for Tondern, 80 miles away. Rutland was not among the pilots; he had been transferred to the Admiralty and assigned to help in the design and construction of future aircraft carriers.

At Tondern, Zeppelin pilot Horst Treusch von Buttlar-Brandenfels was one of the first to see the planes. "They were flying high," he said of the Camels, "but while they were still small specks I saw them begin to plane down. It was all over in a minute or two after that. Part of them headed for one shed and part for the other. Down they came, till they seemed to be going to ram the sheds. Then, one after another, they flattened out and passed lengthwise over their targets at a height of about forty metres, kicking loose bombs as they went."

German antiaircraft guns proved ineffective, and Buttlar watched as a

Camel bore down on a gun that was firing at it. "Banking steeply, round he came, dived straight at the battery, letting go a bomb when he was no more than fifteen metres above it. Then he waved his hand and dashed off after the other machines, which were already scattering to avoid the German planes beginning to converge on them from all directions. It was one of the finest examples of nerve I ever saw."

Tondern lay in ruins. The two Zeppelin sheds, along with the airships they had sheltered, were demolished, and dirigibles would rarely harass British ships again. The net cost to the attackers was one pilot, presumed lost at sea. Some of the rest were picked up after ditching successfully at sea; others flew on to neutral Denmark and internment.

The Tondern raid confirmed Admiral Beatty's hope that ship-based aircraft could be used for attack missions as well as for reconnaissance. Unfortunately, since the *Furious* could not recover her planes on board, the ship was a one-shot weapon that had to steam home to England to be reloaded. Thus Beatty looked forward to the arrival of the new flush-decked carrier *Argus,* which began fleet trials in October 1918.

The *Argus* carried Sopwith Camel fighters to command the air and scout planes to locate enemy warships. But Beatty's highest expectations were for the carrier's 18 new Sopwith Cuckoo torpedo planes, which he was eager to throw into an attack on the German fleet at its anchorage in Germany. He would not get his wish. In November 1918, before the *Argus* could complete her trials, the War ended.

With the signing of the Armistice, the Royal Navy had the only aircraft carrier in the world, and with two more carriers, the *Eagle* and the *Hermes,* under construction, Britain had a commanding lead in naval aviation. But it would not keep this position. Over the next two decades, Britain's capacity to conduct air warfare from the sea stagnated.

There were two main reasons. The admirals who ran the Royal Navy were for the most part battleship men; they had little enthusiasm for aircraft carriers. Worse yet, the Navy had lost control of its aircraft in April 1918, when the Royal Naval Air Service was absorbed into the newly formed Royal Air Force. The men in charge of the RAF had little regard for naval aviation and for nearly 20 years sent the Navy's expanding carrier fleet insufficient numbers of planes, most of which were unsuitable for sea duty and manned by pilots of little distinction.

Not until 1937 would the Navy finally retrieve its air arm from the RAF. During the intervening years, aircraft carriers assigned to Britain's fleets around the world were capable of little more than ancillary service to the ships with the big guns. It was left to the United States and Japan, facing each other across the Pacific Ocean, to forge the aircraft carrier into the awesome offensive weapon that it would become.

The Americans would pick up the development of carrier warfare where the British left off, but first they had to catch up. The senior admirals of the U.S. Navy had not taken advantage of Eugene Ely's pioneering landing and takeoff from a ship in 1911. Like the British, they preferred

Britain's H.M.S. Furious, the world's first fully decked aircraft carrier, steams through the North Sea in July 1918 with two flights of Sopwith Camel fighters—six of them visible on the ship's bow. Their target: German Zeppelins in their enormous sheds at Tondern, Germany (opposite).

to use seaplanes, deploying them at Vera Cruz during the Mexican Revolution in 1914 and against the Germans during World War I. Aircraft found their way onto American battleships and cruisers, using takeoff decks like those of the British. But the U.S. Navy did introduce an important new device: a catapult to launch pontoon-equipped fighters and scout planes from the warships. At the end of the War, the United States had no plans for a carrier like Britain's *Argus,* even though several American pilots had observed wartime air operations aboard the *Furious* and urged the Navy Department to launch a carrier to scout for the fleet, command the air above it and attack the enemy.

The vision of these prescient pilots got a boost from an unexpected quarter—General William "Billy" Mitchell, who had returned from the war in Europe to open a personal crusade for an autonomous air force. Uninterested in scout planes as eyes for the fleet, Mitchell focused on the offensive potential of seaborne aircraft, calling for three passenger liners to be converted into a carrier attack force independent of the fleet and

Struck by marauding planes from the Furious, a Zeppelin shed erupts in smoke and flame. Two German airships were destroyed in the course of the assault, and one historian wrote that "the Germans lived in constant fear of a similar attack on one of the other bases."

armed with fighters and planes to carry bombs and torpedoes. And if the Navy would not build them, said Mitchell, then the Army—or better yet an independent air force—should.

At this point, the Navy was a step ahead of Mitchell in having a carrier built and several steps behind him in imagining how it might be used. The Navy had already decided to convert the collier *Jupiter* into an 11,500-ton carrier, to be named the *Langley*. But the Navy intended to use its planes solely for scouting rather than to attack the enemy.

Captain Thomas T. Craven, Director of Naval Aviation and the fifth officer since Captain Chambers to head the Navy's air arm, oversaw the creation of the *Langley* and at the same time openly battled with Mitchell to keep the Navy in control of its own planes. Though Craven gained the sobriquet "Father of the Flattop," he disclaimed it. "I might be termed the obstetrician attending," he acknowledged, and he gave credit for the new vessel to its prospective executive officer, Commander Kenneth Whiting. With two assistants, Lieutenant Commander Godfrey de Chevalier and Lieutenant Alfred M. Pride, Whiting developed new procedures for launching and recovering planes, and a system of cross-deck arresting wires to stop aircraft as they landed. Not all their innovations were practical, however. Homing pigeons, intended for dispatch to the ship in case of radio malfunctions in the planes, achieved little more distinction than that of providing fresh squab for dinner.

As work on the *Langley* inched forward, Billy Mitchell goaded the Navy into supplying captured German warships as targets for bombing trials off the Virginia coast in July 1921. Army and Navy aircraft easily sent to the bottom three submarines, a cruiser and a destroyer before the main event took place: the sinking of the battleship *Ostfriesland* by 1,100- and 2,000-pound bombs dropped by Army Martin bombers. Mitchell subsequently proclaimed the obsolescence of battleships in the face of air attack, but the Navy had already intensified the development of its air arm—although not so much to replace battleships as to protect them. Six months earlier it had proposed a Bureau of Aeronautics to give naval aviation equal standing with the Navy's other major interests—ships, propulsion systems and weapons.

The bureau's first chief was Rear Admiral William A. Moffett, a soft-spoken, stately South Carolinian. Though fresh from command of the battleship *Mississippi,* he revealed himself to be a tougher proponent of naval aviation than Craven. While Mitchell publicly called for an independent air force, Moffett quietly fed to key Congressmen and the press facts and figures that argued for the creation of a strong naval air arm. For months, progress was glacially slow. Then, success.

To defuse an intensifying naval arms race between the United States, Great Britain and Japan, Charles Evans Hughes, the United States Secretary of State, convened the Washington Naval Conference late in 1921. The resulting Washington Treaty limited capital ship and carrier tonnage in the ratio of 5 for the United States, 5 for Great Britain, and 3 for Japan. The total tonnage for aircraft carriers was 135,000 tons for each of the two English-speaking powers and 81,000 tons for Japan. Maximum size for new carriers was 27,000 tons, except that each navy was allowed two heavy carriers displacing up to 33,000 tons apiece.

To comply with the capital ship provisions of the Treaty, the U.S. Navy had to scrap seven battle cruisers then being built. Moffett saw his chance. He argued that two of the ships should be completed as aircraft carriers—the *Lexington* and the *Saratoga,* each with a complement of 72 aircraft. The battleship admirals agreed, since converting the ships to carriers was preferable to scrapping them. Japan transformed the battle cruiser *Akagi* and the battleship *Kaga* into carriers, which also carried 72 planes each. But the British settled for smaller conversions, turning two cruisers into the 42-plane flattops *Courageous* and *Glorious.*

Six weeks after the signing of the Washington Treaty, on March 20, 1922, the tiny *Langley* was commissioned as America's first aircraft carrier and assigned the hull designation CV-1, *C* standing for carrier and *V* being an arbitrary symbol for heavier-than-air aircraft. But more

A bearded Captain Joseph M. Reeves (left), commander of the U.S. Navy's battle-fleet aircraft squadrons, and Admiral William A. Moffett, director of the Bureau of Aeronautics, observe flight operations aboard the aircraft carrier U.S.S. Langley in 1926. Working separately but with equal determination, Moffett and Reeves—who would soon be promoted to admiral—founded the American naval air arm.

than two and a half years would pass before Commander Whiting and his team on the *Langley* had ironed out hundreds of operational details and the carrier was ready to join the fleet. Whiting approved the language for new commands—such as "Pilots, man your planes"—and a variety of new signals. A white flag at the aft end of the flight deck, for example, signified that planes could land; a red flag warned them away. Pilots had to be trained to fly on and off the *Langley* in seven different types of Navy planes. The position of the landing signal officer, or LSO, was established; he stood next to the flight deck and coached pilots into position for a successful landing. The ship spent much of 1923 in the Navy yard at Norfolk, Virginia, undergoing modifications of her catapult and arresting gear suggested by her initial trials. Then she headed to sea for tests.

In January 1924, a large portion of the U.S. Navy's ships were staging a mock attack against the Panama Canal in an exercise called Fleet Problem II. It was the second of what would be a two-decade series of practice battles designed to hone the skills of America's seagoing combat forces. Since the *Langley* was not yet formally a ship of the fleet, her assignment was to observe the exercise for ways in which she might be useful in future fleet problems. The *Langley's* captain, who knew nothing about aviation, might have been content to be a spectator on the sidelines, but not Commander Whiting. As the officer in charge of air operations, he launched mock torpedo attacks against battleships anchored at Colón, at the Atlantic end of the canal, then after the exercise he submitted an analysis of his air operations to the board of officers charged with reviewing the results of the exercise.

The response was disappointing. The exercise critique mentioned aircraft only to complain about low-level stunting and to assert that aerial torpedo attacks would fail in shallow-water ports like Colón. Torpedoes dived too deep before leveling off and would plow into the seabed. Nonetheless, the next five years were banner ones for the U.S. Navy's air arm. In 1925 the Morrow Board, a panel of aviation authorities under Dwight W. Morrow, a respected statesman, affirmed the importance of aircraft carriers under Navy control.

The Navy placed Captain Joseph M. Reeves in charge of its carrier-borne planes, naming him Commander Aircraft Squadrons Battle Fleet. Reeves, who had been on the faculty at the Naval War College, a bastion of battleship philosophy, hoisted his pennant aboard the *Langley* at San Diego in the fall of 1925. He wanted carriers to attack, not merely to reconnoiter. He urged development of new techniques such as dive bombing. To increase the *Langley's* offensive punch he experimented with spotting, or parking, planes topside as well as below on the hangar deck. As a result, he gradually increased the ship's capacity from eight to 42 planes (36 fighter-bombers and six scouts).

But the *Langley* soon became obsolete, overshadowed by the long-awaited *Lexington* and *Saratoga* when they finally joined the fleet in 1928. The ships were huge. Each displaced 36,000 tons, although

Freshly overhauled at Washington State's Puget Sound Navy Yard, the carriers (from top) Lexington, Saratoga and Langley await new orders after rigorous war games near the Panama Canal in 1929. The three ships formed America's first carrier fleet and could carry some 200 planes.

official American publications listed them at 33,000 tons so they would seem to conform to the Washington Treaty. Both had flight decks almost 900 feet long and island superstructures rising from the starboard side. Reeves made room on each ship for 90 planes divided into squadrons by function: scouting planes, dive bombers, torpedo planes and fighters. The Navy named each squadron by a letter code indicating its purpose and numbered each type of squadron consecutively. Thus the *Lexington,* for example, had a fighter squadron designated VF-3B: *V* for heavier than air, *F* for fighter and *B* for the bombing role that the fighters could assume. The 3 meant that the unit was the third fighter squadron formed by the Navy. Informally the squadron was known as Fighting 3. Similarly, scouting squadrons carried the designation VS. The *Lexington's* dive bombers were organized into VB squadrons and torpedo units were labeled VT. This new system of squadron nomenclature was adopted for all carrier units, though in 1937 the Navy dropped the letter after the number in the name of the squadron.

The *Lexington* and *Saratoga* gave Reeves the punch he needed to demonstrate the offensive power of carriers. His opportunity came in January 1929, with Fleet Problem IX. The exercise plan called for an "enemy" force designated the Black Fleet to attack the Panama Canal from the Pacific Ocean. The canal was to be defended by another force, the Blue Fleet, which began the exercise with its ships concentrated in the Atlantic. The seaplane tender *Aroostook* (substituting for the *Langley,* then undergoing an overhaul) and the *Saratoga* were assigned to the Black Fleet; the *Lexington* was to help defend the canal. As usual in these exercises, the carriers were expected to work closely with the battleships of their side. But Reeves had other ideas.

The *Saratoga,* with a top speed of 34 knots, could steam circles around 23-knot battleships, and Reeves believed that the *Saratoga,* called a fast carrier because of her speed, should operate independently of the battleship formation. So he went to Admiral William V. Pratt, the progressive officer who commanded the Black Fleet, and asked for permission to change the operations plan, which tied the carriers to the battleships as they attempted to approach the canal and bombard it with their long-range guns. Instead, he recommended that the *Saratoga* be detached for an independent sneak air attack on the canal. After some initial reluctance, Pratt approved.

As the exercise commenced, the defending Blue Fleet sent a battleship division accompanied by the *Lexington* and an escort of destroyers through the canal to the Pacific to thwart Black Fleet's approach. But less than 24 hours after passing through the canal, the force ran smack into Black's battleships under circumstances in which the *Lexington* could easily have been sunk in a real battle. In order to keep the war game going, the umpires ruled her only damaged and limited her speed to 18 knots. Meanwhile, the *Saratoga,* escorted by a Black Fleet cruiser, ran south to the vicinity of the Galápagos Islands, separating herself from the Black Fleet's battleships. During the night, she altered course and steamed at high speed toward Panama. Then, two hours before dawn, she launched a mock strike of 70 aircraft. The planes struck without warning in an attack deemed so effective by the referees that they ruled the locks at the Pacific end of the canal destroyed. Though the air raid was a success, the day ended badly for the *Saratoga.* Her planes returned from their mission to find that she had been discovered by the enemy and counted as sunk by the referees.

The *Saratoga's* performance changed naval warfare; she had demonstrated that a speedy aircraft carrier could independently attack enemy shore installations with devastating consequences. True, she had been ruled sunk, and refined tactics would be necessary to protect carriers in the future. But battleships had been lost, too, and their guns had not equaled the damage caused by the *Saratoga's* planes.

None of this was lost on the Black Fleet commander, Admiral Pratt, who praised the ship and its fliers. "Gentlemen," he said in his post-exercise critique, "you have witnessed the most brilliantly conceived and most effectively executed naval operation in our history. I expect to fly my flag in the *Saratoga* on our return cruise north, partly as a badge of distinction but mostly because I want to know what makes the aircraft squadrons tick." The very next year Pratt was in a position to make sure

Admiral Isoroku Yamamoto, commander of the Japanese Combined Fleet, stands on the bridge of his flagship, the Nagato, in this painting. Yamamoto, an early supporter of aircraft carriers, had lost two fingers of his left hand as an ensign at the Battle of Tsushima in the 1904-1905 Russo-Japanese War.

they kept ticking; he was named Chief of Naval Operations, the man in charge of running the Navy. During his tenure, the carrier became for the first time the nucleus of an independent offensive unit in the fleet.

The *Saratoga's* performance was a matter of acute interest to Japan. Though the Japanese had no inclination at this time to fight the United States, they prudently kept a close watch on U.S. naval developments. In Japan as elsewhere during the early 20th Century, the battleship reigned supreme. After all, battleships of Japan's Combined Fleet, the glorious Rengo Kantai, had beaten the Russian fleet in the Battle of Tsushima in 1905, toward the end of the Russo-Japanese War.

But following the lead of the British, whose Navy they greatly admired, Japanese admirals proposed a Naval Air Service in 1912. The

Lieutenant Commander Minoru Genda, a principal planner of the attack on Pearl Harbor, exudes steely determination in this 1941 photograph. Under the orders of Admiral Yamamoto (opposite), Genda plotted tactics for the Japanese carrier force.

next year a Navy transport ship was converted into a seaplane tender, and shortly after the beginning of World War I, in which Japan fought on the Allied side against Germany, planes from this ship scouted and bombed the German-held city of Tsingtao in China.

Nevertheless, Japanese strategy after the War favored seaplanes and land-based aircraft over shipborne planes. Should an enemy attack by sea, the Japanese planned to chip away at the opposing fleet until it was inferior to the battleships of the Rengo Kantai. Then a decisive Tsushima-style surface engagement, fought within range of the Navy's shore-based aircraft and seaplanes, would settle the issue.

But a few farsighted admirals realized the need for *koku bokan,* literally mother ships for aircraft, if for no other purpose than reconnaissance. In 1919 Japan began construction of the tiny 7,500-ton carrier *Hosho.* In 1921, the same year that the Washington Conference met to set limits on ship construction, Japan's still minuscule naval air arm welcomed an advisory mission of 30 naval aviators from Britain. Less than two years later, the Japanese began converting the *Akagi* and the *Kaga* into aircraft carriers. The *Akagi* was completed in 1927; a year later the *Kaga* joined the fleet. Each displaced more than 30,000 tons.

Japanese progress in naval aviation was remarkable—and all the more so because during the 1920s the Imperial Navy lacked an advocate of American Admiral Moffett's rank and influence to forge the carriers into an offensive force in their own right. But a Japanese officer who would fill this role was soon to rise to prominence. He was Captain Isoroku Yamamoto. As a young ensign, he had fought in the Battle of Tsushima. He studied at Harvard after World War I and later became second-in-command of the Kasumigaura naval air training station, where he learned to fly. By the time of Fleet Problem IX and the *Saratoga's* simulated attack on the Panama Canal, Yamamoto had served two years as naval attaché to Japan's embassy in Washington, D.C., and had been assigned command of the *Akagi,* Japan's largest carrier.

One of Yamamoto's protégés was a brilliant young pilot, Lieutenant Minoru Genda. He first served under Yamamoto in 1933 and marveled at the way the admiral "tersely pointed out the essence of problems under discussion. His words revealed far more important things than anyone ever thought of" during meetings held to plan exercises.

The 1930s were tumultuous years for Japan. The government had begun to exert a measure of control over the historically autonomous Army, in part by refusing appropriations that the Army had sought. The generals resented what they saw as an intrusion on the Army's traditional independence. They had been accustomed to reporting to the Emperor and deriving their authority directly from him, and they were determined not to be shackled by a pack of bureaucrats.

To regain their stature, the generals plotted to involve Japan in a war reasoning that hostilities would restore the Army to a position of dominance. In 1931, without even notifying Japan's civilian government, the Army took over the Chinese province of Manchuria. Japanese troops had been stationed there to protect Japanese business interests since 1905; now the Army announced the annexation of the 440,000-square-mile area and forced the Japanese government to accept the *fait accompli*. Some of the few politicians who spoke against the Army were subsequently assassinated by fanatic young officers. Then in 1937, using as a pretext a clash between Chinese soldiers and Japanese troops posted at Peking since the Boxer Rebellion in 1900, Japan's Army launched an all-out war against China.

Until this point, the Japanese Navy had been only peripherally involved with its country's rampaging ground forces; the Army had little use for warships, and the Navy was unenthusiastic about the Army's adventures. But now the Navy responded to the war brewing in China by sending the carriers *Akagi* and *Kaga* to attack Chinese forces near Hangchow. As soon as captured Chinese airfields became available, other Navy fighter and bomber units relieved the carrier aircraft.

American sympathies lay with the Chinese, but the United States was officially neutral. And America remained neutral even when Japanese naval aircraft sank the United States gunboat *Panay* in the Yangtze River on December 12, 1937, while she was escorting American oil barges from the battle zone. Whether or not the attack was an accident, American determination to avoid war made it easy to accept a prompt Japanese apology and more than two million dollars in restitution.

If the *Panay* incident did not steer Japan onto a collision course with the United States, then the outbreak of war in Europe almost two years later did. Japan saw a golden chance, while the nations of Europe were at one anothers' throats, to strip them of their Asian colonies, rich in raw materials that resource-poor Japan badly needed. To protect her conquests, Japan would also have to occupy islands far out in the Pacific, forming a buffer zone that could absorb American retaliation, for the Americans would surely come. Among the islands Japan would have to take were the Philippines, then an American commonwealth.

Hoping to deter the Japanese from further depredations in China, President Franklin D. Roosevelt in mid-1940 ordered the U.S. Pacific Fleet from its traditional base in San Diego to Pearl Harbor on the Hawaiian island of Oahu. By then it had become clear to war-minded Japanese that if they were going to fight the United States, the sooner they got on with it the better. America had launched a warship-building program that aimed to double the size of the Navy. Japanese naval superiority in the Pacific would soon be reduced and ultimately eliminated. Moreover, the United States had begun a program of trade restrictions calculated to dissuade Japan from its course of aggression. The time when it might be possible for Japan to defeat the United States seemed to be slipping away. Thus to many Japanese, war began to appear inevitable—except in the unlikely event that they could extract an agreement from the Americans to let Japan work her will in Asia.

Japanese strategy for meeting a threat from the east had changed little since World War I; the central plan called for picking away at the

U.S. fleet as it crossed the Pacific and then crushing it in a decisive battle hundreds of miles east of Japan. But Yamamoto, who had risen to the rank of admiral and in 1939 assumed command of the Combined Fleet, had a new plan. He was against going to war with the United States, but if war did come he wanted to surprise the U.S. fleet at anchor in Pearl Harbor and, before it could become a menace, destroy it in one blow.

Japan would soon have the aircraft carriers to do the job. Since commissioning the *Kaga* and the *Akagi* in the late 1920s, the Japanese had completed or started six new carriers. They ranged in displacement from the diminutive *Ryujo* at 10,600 tons to the fast carriers *Shokaku* and *Zuikaku*, each displacing nearly 26,000 tons. Altogether, Japanese carriers could carry more than 350 aircraft and totaled more than twice the 81,000 tons that Japan would have been allowed by its naval limitation treaties with the United States and Britain—but Japan had formally withdrawn from the agreements in 1936.

Japan's participation in the agreements had been undermined by the "fleet faction" of the Japanese Navy. It consisted of battleship admirals

Lying majestically at the Kure Naval Arsenal, Japan's 15,900-ton carrier Soryu undergoes a refitting in early 1937. Launched little more than a year earlier, the Soryu was the third Japanese flattop—the much smaller Hosho and Ryujo had preceded it—designed and built as an aircraft carrier from the keel up.

Crewmen aboard the Japanese aircraft carrier Kaga prepare warplanes for naval exercises in May 1937, just two months before the beginning of the war with China. These fighters, dive bombers and attack planes were among the last biplanes to be used on Japanese carriers.

who had supported the Army's occupation of Manchuria in 1931, who did not shrink from war with the United States and who regarded aircraft carriers as mere support vessels for the fleet's battleships. Yamamoto belonged to the "treaty faction" of naval officers who opposed war with the United States on the ground that Japan could never win. But he also believed that aircraft carriers would be the arbiters of future sea battles with any opponent and he worked diligently to overcome technical deficiencies in Japanese planes and to develop naval aviation tactics.

During fleet exercises in the spring of 1940, Yamamoto used torpedo planes against ships so effectively that his own chief of staff, Rear Admiral Shigeru Fukudome, remarked that "the time is now ripe for a decisive fleet engagement with aerial torpedo attacks as the main striking power." Yamamoto agreed, musing that even a surprise attack on the U.S. fleet anchored at Pearl Harbor might succeed.

Yamamoto realized that there were many problems to be solved before the plan could work. Japanese escort ships, designed to support a battleship duel near Japan, lacked the range to reach Hawaii without

Poised for combat, Japanese Navy pilots huddle on the Kaga's flight deck for some last-minute instructions before they take off on a raid against China in August of 1937. The markings on their life jackets identify the fliers as crewmen from the Kaga and name their flight units.

refueling at sea, a technique the Japanese had not yet perfected. Japanese torpedoes, like the Americans', dived too deep before leveling off to be used in shallow ports like Pearl Harbor. Moreover, Yamamoto's carriers as yet had no way to coordinate mass air attacks while maintaining radio silence, an essential element of surprise. But Yamamoto was far from discouraged. Indeed, in November 1940, an event in Europe made him all the more sure that the American fleet could be mortally wounded before it ever put to sea: British carrier-based torpedo planes surprised the Italian fleet at Taranto with devastating results *(page 42).*

Yamamato drew up his own proposal for a moonlight or dawn attack on the U.S. fleet at Pearl Harbor. To Admiral Fukudome he said, "I want a flier whose past career has not influenced him in conventional operations to analyze the chances for success." He chose Rear Admiral Takijiro Onishi, a member of the Naval General Staff with broad experience in the use of airpower. Onishi began his study in January 1941, working with Minoru Genda, who now held the rank of commander.

Coincidentally, Genda had recently solved one of the major prob-

Britain's Illustrious, seen here shortly before her attack on Taranto, was the world's first fully armored carrier. Her steel flight deck was three inches thick.

Attacking pilots from the British aircraft carrier Illustrious wheel over the battered Italian fleet at Taranto harbor in this painting by artist Laurence Bagley.

An epochal display of carrier power

Under the cover of darkness on November 11, 1940, a dozen Fairey Swordfish biplanes flew off the deck of the British carrier *Illustrious* and headed across the Mediterranean Sea toward the Italian mainland, about 170 miles to the northwest. The frail aircraft were on their way to attack an Italian fleet moored at Taranto harbor, a naval stronghold that bristled with antiaircraft guns. The raid would be a stern test of the effectiveness of aircraft carriers as naval weapons; never before had carrier-based aircraft struck a fleet of warships.

Led by Lieutenant Commander Kenneth Williamson, the 12 warplanes—six armed with torpedoes, four with bombs and two with a mixed load of bombs plus flares for lighting up the targets—split up as they approached Taranto, hoping to confuse the antiaircraft gunners. About an hour behind them came a second wave of nine planes from the *Illustrious.*

Braving a ceaseless barrage of antiaircraft fire, the Swordfish swarmed over the enemy anchorage and disabled three battleships, a cruiser and two destroyers—half of Italy's fleet strength. The attackers lost only two of their planes.

The day after this devastating attack, the remainder of the Italian fleet steamed north to take refuge in Naples, yielding the Mediterranean sea-lanes, at an early and critical point in the War, to the British Royal Navy. The worth of aircraft carriers could hardly have been more convincingly demonstrated.

lems facing the Hawaiian operation, as it was now known: how to coordinate an air strike and maintain radio silence. Ironically his inspiration was a newsreel he saw in October 1940 of four U.S. carriers steaming in formation. Japan's practice was to operate carriers only in groups of two and widely dispersed. With this dispersion tactic, two-carrier divisions would be separated by more than 100 miles yet would be able to concentrate 80 to 100 planes over the enemy fleet. Genda could not get the American ships off his mind. Then, when he was stepping off a streetcar one day, the idea suddenly struck him that the operations of four or even more carriers, launching from the same cruising formation, could be coordinated by visual signals, without recourse to radio.

"The weakness of this tactic," he later observed, "would be vulnerability of the formation to enemy air attack, but defensive fighters over the whole carrier group and the coordinated antiaircraft fire by the carriers and their escorts would be far more effective than dispersing the ships and defensive fighters." In the end, Genda suggested that dispersion tactics be used in sea battles with enemy carriers, when flexibility would be crucial, but that flattops form up 7,000 meters apart in a tight box formation for attacking shore targets—and anchored ships.

In April 1941, Onishi and Genda concluded that the attack ought to succeed, provided that the element of surprise could be maintained and that torpedoes could be made to work in the 45-foot shallows of Pearl Harbor. The Naval General Staff did not agree. They thought the idea too risky. But Yamamoto immediately began contingency plans for such an operation. He had already reorganized the Combined Fleet, assigning most of the carriers to the new First Air Fleet. Vice Admiral Chuichi Nagumo, not a pilot but a prudent senior officer, was given command; his shortcomings as an aviator would be more than compensated for by his chief of staff, Rear Admiral Ryunosuke Kusaka, a pilot who had commanded both the *Hosho* and *Akagi,* and by Genda, who would serve as the fleet's air operations officer.

Late in the summer Yamamoto, who dreamed of leading the raid himself if someone could take his place as Commander in Chief of the Combined Fleet, intensified torpedo drill and had the carriers practice attacks from the box formation. To give the raid the best chance of success, Yamamoto recalled half his veteran fighter pilots from China.

As the summer wore on, the efforts of diplomats seemed less and less likely to prevent a collision between Japan and the United States. In July, President Roosevelt expanded the trade embargo to include oil. Japan had to acquire a new source for this crucial item immediately, and on September 6, 1941, began to plan the invasion of the oil-rich Dutch East Indies, as well as rubber-producing British Malaya. To protect the sea-lanes, the Philippines would also have to be taken. Commencement of war with America would then be only a matter of time.

There was still no certainty, however, that Yamamoto's plan for attacking the U.S. fleet would be approved by the Naval Staff. In mid-September, in fact, the prospects for the plan seemed bleak. When the

Hawaiian operation was the subject of a war game on a tabletop map of Pearl Harbor at the Naval Staff College, some of the carriers that approached Hawaii in broad daylight were ruled sunk by an American counterattack. However, none of the carriers advancing under cover of darkness were even spotted. Even so, the Naval General Staff had grave reservations about risking Japan's carriers in such a raid. The war game also made disbelievers of Nagumo, Onishi and even Kusaka, the very men who would have to make the operation work.

Only Genda retained enthusiasm for the plan—and of course Yamamoto, who thought the carrier losses in the war game could be avoided by launching the raid before dawn. Yamamoto refused to give in. If Japan insisted on the folly of war with the United States, then the Hawaiian operation must be approved, he told them; if it was rejected, he would resign. The Naval Staff acquiesced but insisted that Yamamoto remain in home waters with the battleships while Nagumo and Kusaka led the First Air Fleet to Pearl Harbor.

In the meantime the First Air Fleet had concentrated at Kagoshima Bay, a Pearl Harbor look-alike in southern Japan, to practice the mission. Only the key planners knew the real object of these preparations, and only they were allowed to study a large plaster model of Pearl Harbor on board the *Akagi.* Commander Mitsuo Fuchida, on the staff of the Third Carrier Division, was ordered to the flagship *Akagi.* "Now don't be alarmed, Fuchida," his old friend Genda announced, "but we want you to lead our air force in the event we attack Pearl Harbor!" Exhilarated, Fuchida drilled his pilots relentlessly. Sixteen-inch naval gun shells were modified into armor-piercing bombs. In September, the *Kaga* overcame the logistical problems of the long voyage by demonstrating that she could refuel while under way. Finally, the puzzle of making the torpedoes run shallow was solved when Genda and Captain Fumio Aiko fitted wooden stabilizing fins to them early in October.

The attack was set for December 7, Hawaii time, to take advantage of a bright moon for a predawn launch. The 7th was also a Sunday, and the U.S. fleet habitually spent Sundays in port. The Japanese hoped to find in Pearl Harbor all eight of the Pacific Fleet's battleships plus four carriers: the *Lexington* and three flattops completed after Japan withdrew from the naval limitations agreement—the *Yorktown,* the *Enterprise* and the *Hornet.* The *Saratoga* was being refitted in San Diego.

To avoid detection by merchant ships, the Japanese planned to reach Hawaii by steaming across the isolated northern Pacific and approaching their target from the northwest. Sailing one by one to preserve their deadly secret, the six carriers made their way to a secret rendezvous at Hitokappu Bay in the Kurile Islands north of Japan. On November 26 the Pearl Harbor striking force set out. In addition to the flattops the force included two battleships, three cruisers, nine destroyers and three submarines. Eight tankers refueled them twice in unusually calm seas. Some of the tankers then returned to Japan; others took up station to refuel the warships after the attack.

Admiral Nagumo fretted about the uncertainties of the voyage, but his pilots, when at last they were told what their mission would be, knew only excitement. At 11:30 a.m. on December 6, the force began its final run to reach the launch point some 200 miles north of Pearl Harbor before dawn on the 7th. Then came encouraging news from a Japanese spy in Hawaii. All the American battleships were in port and there were "no balloons, no torpedo-defense nets deployed around battleships. No indications observed from enemy radio activity that ocean patrol flights are being made in Hawaiian area." But there was bad news about the U.S. carriers. "*Lexington* left harbor yesterday," the report continued. "*Enterprise* is also thought to be operating at sea with her planes on board. All carriers and heavy cruisers are at sea."

No carriers in port! Admiral Nagumo discussed the situation with his staff, one of whom suggested that the eight battleships were a rewarding target even if the carriers were away. Nagumo agreed and made the decision to attack even though the carriers might escape.

The pilots arose in the middle of the night for a traditional battle breakfast of red rice, fish and chestnuts. At 5:30 a.m. two seaplanes were launched from cruisers to reconnoiter Pearl Harbor. These scouts, who were to report the latest disposition of American ships and the weather at Pearl Harbor, were the only reconnaissance aircraft sent out by this powerful armada. They would radio their reports back to the planes that followed. Sending only two scouts could have been a risky decision had the American carriers been in the vicinity. Fortunately for Nagumo they were elsewhere. *Lexington* and *Enterprise* were away delivering planes to Marine outposts on Midway and Wake Island and the other two, Japanese intelligence to the contrary, were not even in the Pacific. The *Yorktown* was assigned to the Atlantic Fleet and the *Hornet* was on a shakedown cruise in the Caribbean.

After Fuchida had eaten, he went to the *Akagi's* operations room, where he told Admiral Nagumo: "I am ready for the mission."

"I have confidence in you," replied the admiral, and he accompanied Fuchida to the pilots' briefing room to say a last word to the fliers.

Then Fuchida went onto the flight deck, where a message from Yamamoto had been chalked on a blackboard hung from the island. It read: "The rise and fall of the Empire depends on this very campaign. I expect every one of you will fulfill your duties." Fuchida climbed into his torpedo bomber (a Nakajima B5N2 Type 97, called a Kate by the U.S. Navy, which assigned easily pronounced names to Japanese aircraft). Fuchida, flying as a passenger, would direct the attack from the Kate.

At 6:00 a.m., to cheers of "Banzai" from crewmen, the first plane rolled down the pitching deck of the *Akagi*. It was a Mitsubishi A6M2 Zero, a fast maneuverable fighter that the Japanese had designed on the basis of their wartime experience in China. The pilot was Lieutenant Commander Shigeru Itaya, leader of the fighters. With 42 additional Zeros from three carriers, Itaya was to fly top cover for the aircraft assigned to hit the ships in Pearl Harbor.

Vice Admiral Chuichi Nagumo, who led Japan's Pearl Harbor strike force, mans the bridge of his flagship, the Akagi, shortly before the attack. Worried that his carriers would be demolished by an airborne counterassault, Nagumo had been reluctant to accept the assignment.

After the Zeros were launched from the carrier, the first wave of attack planes took off into the overcast. First Fuchida's Kate and 48 others roared into the lowering sky, each carrying one of the armor-piercing bombs made from gun shells. Next, Lieutenant Commander Kakuichi Takahashi of the *Shokaku* led off with a force of 51 dive bombers (Aichi D3A1 Type 99, known to Americans as the Val), each one armed with a bomb weighing about 550 pounds. To complete the first wave, Lieutenant Commander Shigeharu Murata of the *Akagi* took off at the head of 40 torpedo-laden Kates. At 7:15 a.m., a second wave of 170 planes, led by Lieutenant Commander Shigekazu Shimazaki, air group commander of the *Zuikaku,* set course for Oahu. Thirty Zeros remained behind to protect the carriers in case of attack.

In this captured Japanese photograph, America's stricken Pacific Fleet lies helpless at Ford Island in Pearl Harbor during the surprise attack on December 7, 1941. If the Japanese had also bombed the vital oil-tank farm (upper right), the U.S. Pacific Fleet would have been out of action for months.

At 7 a.m. Fuchida, about halfway to the target, picked up a Honolulu weather report of clear skies over Pearl Harbor, took a radio bearing on the signal and adjusted his course. Soon he sighted the white surf breaking on the beaches of Oahu and through the morning haze trained his binoculars on Battleship Row, "at the ships riding peacefully at anchor. One by one I counted them. Yes, the battleships were there all right, eight of them! But our last lingering hope of finding any carriers present was now gone. Not one was to be seen."

Pearl Harbor seemed to be asleep, and Fuchida opened his canopy and fired a flare, a prearranged signal announcing no enemy opposition. Takahashi, leading dive bombers from the *Akagi* and *Kaga,* bored in ahead of the Kates and at 7:55 hit Wheeler and Hickam Army airfields and the Navy air installations at Ford Island, next to which the battleships were moored, their crews just going to morning colors. As the bombs crashed among parked planes, torpedo-plane leader Murata worried that the rising smoke might obscure his targets, so he brought his Kates in quickly at 7:57 for their drops.

White geysers erupted where the torpedoes splashed into the harbor, and their black shapes cut wakes straight toward Battleship Row. New geysers rocketed skyward alongside the hulls of the great ships as the carefully aimed torpedoes found their marks. Too late, the battleships began to throw up antiaircraft fire.

Chief Flight Petty Officer Juzo Mori from the *Soryu* chose not to send his torpedo at the cruiser in front of him on his first pass. "If I were going to die," he remembered thinking as he brought his torpedo bomber around for a second try, "I wanted to know that I had torpedoed at least an American battleship." Swinging into position, he braved the storm of fire to go in low against his new target. "By this time I was hardly conscious of what I was doing," he said. "I was reacting from habit instilled by long training, moving like an automaton. Suddenly the battleship appeared to have leaped forward directly in front of my speeding plane; it towered ahead like a great mountain peak."

As Mori released his torpedo, the plane lurched and faltered as antiaircraft fire struck the wings and fuselage. "My head snapped back," he wrote later, "and I felt as though a heavy beam had struck against my head. But I've got it! A perfect release! And the plane is still flying!" Mori flew directly over the battleship and turned south in order to deceive the Americans into believing the Japanese carriers lay in that direction.

As the torpedo planes completed their runs, Fuchida's bombers leveled off 10,000 feet above Battleship Row, but between the antiaircraft fire and obscuring clouds they could not make out the targets and did not release their bombs. They began a wide circle for a second try while torpedo bombers from the *Kaga* attacked.

Suddenly a terrific explosion of flame and dark red smoke erupted from the row of battleships. A bomb had struck the forward magazine of the battleship *Arizona,* detonating its ammunition; she sank immediately and took more than 1,000 men down with her.

Fuchida now returned with his torpedo bombers and scored several hits. Then Itaya's fighters roared in, strafing ships, ground installations and the several airfields of Oahu. As one of the Zero pilots, Lieutenant Yoshio Shiga from the *Kaga,* pressed home his strafing run on a parked plane at the Marine Corps' Ewa Field a few miles southwest of Battleship Row, he was startled to see a lone Marine in his sights, standing

Caught at anchor by carrier-based Japanese aircraft, the U.S. battleships West Virginia (left) and Tennessee lie ablaze at their Pearl Harbor berths.

foursquare, unflinching, firing his pistol at Shiga's Zero. The Marines, for their part, were amazed at the sight of two low-flying Japanese rear-seat gunners who interrupted their shooting, one to thumb his nose at them, the other to clasp his hands over his head like a prize fighter.

The first wave of attacks was completed shortly after 8:30 a.m., but Commander Fuchida remained over Oahu to assess the damage and observe the second wave, which came in behind Lieutenant Commander Shimazaki at 8:55. Shimazaki personally led 54 level bombers for drops on the airfields at Hickam, Ford Island and Kaneohe. No fewer than 80 dive bombers roared in against targets of opportunity among the ships in the harbor. By this time, a handful of American fighters had taken off to repel the attackers, but they were badly outnumbered by the fighter cover for the second wave. The 36 Zeros in this formation, led by Lieutenant Shindo of the *Akagi,* destroyed a half-dozen American planes in the air and shot up several on the ground. By 10 a.m. the last attack had been completed, and the Japanese planes, to confuse the Americans, flew away in several directions before heading north toward the carriers. Fuchida brought up the rear; he had waited to pick up two straggling Zeros and lead them to safety, since the fighters were not equipped with homing receivers to help them find their carriers.

Fuchida's 353 planes had crippled the U.S. Pacific Fleet. In addition to the *Arizona,* the battleships *California, Oklahoma* and *West Virginia* and a minelayer were sinking or capsized. The *Nevada,* badly damaged, lay aground near the harbor entrance. Three other battleships were damaged, as were three light cruisers, three destroyers and various lesser vessels Nearly 350 aircraft had been wrecked or badly damaged, and 2,403 men were dead or dying. Another 1,178 were wounded.

By 1 p.m. Fuchida's planes were back on their carriers, except for 29 that had been downed with a loss of 55 men. Flushed with success, the pilots wanted to return for another strike, which Fuchida recommended to Admiral Nagumo as a means of enticing the U.S. carriers. He even suggested swinging south of Hawaii to seek a carrier battle instead of retiring to the north. But the oilers were already en route to a prearranged refueling rendezvous, and Nagumo reasoned that little would be gained by another attack. So at 1:30 he ordered his carriers to retire.

The Hawaiian operation had been designed to prevent the U.S. fleet from interfering with the invasion of the Dutch East Indies and Malaya. In this it succeeded, and in the process demonstrated that carrier warfare had arrived. If any major tactical error was made, it was the Japanese failure to destroy Pearl Harbor's repair facilities, power plant, oil tanks, ammunition depot and submarine pens. They had all survived and would hasten the U.S. Navy's recovery.

But the attack on Pearl Harbor, for all the damage it did, was ill conceived. It bought precious little time for the Japanese. It enraged the Americans and unified them in their quest for revenge. And it forced the U.S. Navy, deprived of its battleships, to rely on the very weapon Japan had used to destroy them—the aircraft carrier.

Awaiting their departure from Hitokappu Bay, pilots and antiaircraft gunners stand at combat readiness aboard the carrier Akagi.

Imperial warriors closing for the kill

"The die has already been cast. The arrow has just left the bowstring," a Japanese officer confided to his diary aboard the carrier *Akagi,* flagship of the Pearl Harbor attack force. The date was November 29, 1941, three days after the 31-vessel fleet, including six carriers, had steamed out of Hitokappu Bay, its secret rendezvous in the bleak North Pacific *(left).* During the next seven days, the deadly armada would speed nearly 3,000 miles to the waters off Hawaii and, on December 7, launch a devastating aerial attack on the American fleet at Pearl Harbor.

In keeping with the historic importance of this event, sailors aboard the *Akagi* photographed each step of the voyage in the most minute detail—from their own hammocks that were bound to the carrier's island to shield it from shrapnel to the exhilarating cap waving that greeted a Zero fighter pilot as he prepared for takeoff. These photographs, painstakingly assembled by a Japanese collector after the War and published here for the first time outside Japan, bear witness to the meticulous care and ardent patriotism with which Japan's First Air Fleet set out to strike the first blow against the United States—and succeeded in achieving a stunning carrier victory.

Aerial torpedoes dwarf a lone crewman on the Akagi's flight deck. Special tail fins kept the torpedoes from running aground in the shallow waters of Pearl Harbor.

Constituting one side of a powerful, six-carrier box formation, the Akagi (foreground), Kaga and Zuikaku steam in single file toward Hawaii.

Sailors man the Akagi's superstructure and port gun deck, keeping watch for enemy vessels. "Thank God, they still seem unaware of our advance!" wrote the officer in charge of flight operations.

Beside the Akagi's hammock-clad island, crewmen prepare to pull out the chocks from a Zero ready for takeoff on X-day, December 7.

Jubilant sailors wave their caps and shout "Banzai" as the pilot of a Zero begins his takeoff run down the carrier's flight deck.

Silhouetted against the morning sky, a Nakajima B5N2 heads for Hawaii armed with a 1,760-pound armor-piercing bomb.

Waved in for a landing by a flight control officer (right foreground), a torpedo bomber returns from the attack on Pearl Harbor.

Savoring the day's victory, an exhausted pilot studies maps that estimate the damage inflicted on American planes at Pearl Harbor by the first wave of attackers. The three large symbols below the maps represent the number of battleships believed sunk.

2

Blunting the Japanese onslaught

"I guarantee to put up a tough fight for the first six months," Admiral Yamamoto had told the Japanese Prime Minister more than a year before war with the United States began, "but I have absolutely no confidence as to what might happen if it went on for two or three years." And indeed for the guaranteed six months it seemed that nothing could stop Japan.

Following the attack on Pearl Harbor, Japanese forces swept through the Pacific like a typhoon. In the Central Pacific, Yamamoto's carriers abetted Japanese Marines as they pried Americans from Wake Island, then helped dislodge the Dutch from the Netherlands East Indies. As the Japanese Army pushed into Southeast Asia, the carriers kept the Allies at bay with attacks on the Australian-held port and airfields at Rabaul, New Britain, on Port Darwin in Australia itself, and on British bases in Ceylon. The Rising Sun unfurled over the Philippines and Malaya as invading Japanese forces overwhelmed meager Allied resistance. By April 1942 much of New Guinea had fallen and Rabaul was in Japanese hands. Ultimately, Japan planned to extend her dominance as far east as Samoa *(map, pages 62-63)*, thereby isolating Australia and preventing the Allies from using that country as a base for counterattacks.

Japan's relentless advances endowed the Rising Sun with an aura of invincibility that glowed brighter with each island conquest, with each Allied garrison driven into the sea. Before long the Japanese came to look upon their new splendor as a divine destiny fulfilled; at last they seemed on the threshhold of dominating the whole of the East, as foretold in ancient Shinto scriptures.

Perhaps the prophecy had described a more distant future than the spring of 1942, for Japan's supremacy was about to be challenged by the U.S. Pacific Fleet. Initially the Americans would jab tentatively at Japan's new forward outposts. But early in May, the two nations would clash in a naval battle such as the world had never seen, one in which the opposing fleets would never sight each other as carrierborne aircraft took the contest across hundreds of miles of open sea.

To grapple with the Japanese, the United States had but four flattops. The *Yorktown* and *Hornet* had joined the *Lexington* and *Enterprise* in

Spearheading Japan's rapid advance into the Southwest Pacific, a Navy Aichi dive bomber leads an attack on the harbor at Rabaul, New Britain, shortly before the city was captured in January 1942.

Tinted areas on this map of the Pacific Ocean represent Japan's territories in the spring of 1942, the high point of her fortunes in World War II.

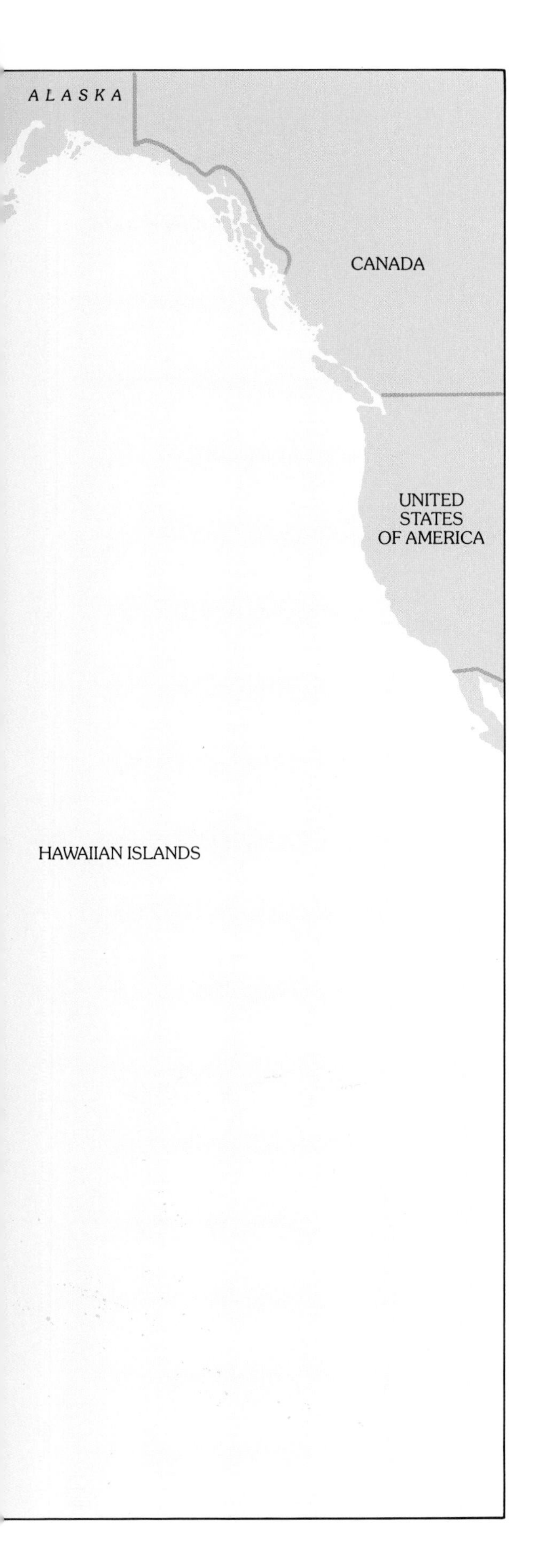

the Pacific. The *Saratoga* had suffered damage from a submarine torpedo on January 11, 1942, while on patrol southwest of Hawaii and was laid up for repairs. Opposing the American carriers were Japan's six veterans of the Pearl Harbor operation. These large flattops of both sides were roughly equal in striking power, and with only negligible differences in size and speed. But the American ships enjoyed one distinct advantage: They had radar to warn of the approach of enemy planes. Japanese radar was too primitive for shipboard use and would remain inferior to the U.S. Navy's throughout the War. Counterbalancing this advantage, Japan had, in addition to the larger aircraft carriers, the light carriers *Hosho* and *Ryujo,* built in the 1920s and 1930s, as well as two new ones, the *Zuiho* and *Shoho,* converted from submarine tenders. Thus Japan actually had 10 carriers, large and small, arrayed against the four American vessels.

Moreover, the Japanese planes and pilots were generally superior to those of the United States Pacific Fleet. The American Navy's torpedo-bomber, the Douglas TBD Devastator, had entered service as a radically advanced all-metal monoplane in 1937, but by 1942 it had become obsolete. With an unimpressive top speed of some 200 miles per hour, it carried a slow-running aerial torpedo that, if it hit the target, often failed to explode. The Navy was rushing into production a replacement for the Devastator, but the first deliveries to the fleet were not expected for weeks. A new torpedo was many months away. For the Americans, the situation in dive bombers was brighter. The Douglas SBD Dauntless, also used as a scout plane, was clearly a superior aircraft. Stable and easy to fly in its 276-mile-per-hour, 70-degree dive, it could carry a payload of 1,200 pounds.

The ability of the torpedo planes and dive bombers to execute successful attacks against enemy ships depended largely on the capacity of the Grumman F4F Wildcat fighter to fend off Japan's magnificent Zero. In the Wildcat, the Navy had "a little beer bottle of a plane with a battery of .50-caliber guns in its tiny wings," as one pilot said. It compared favorably with the Zero in firepower but was slower—318 miles per hour to the Zero's 331. With more armor than the Zero, self-sealing fuel tanks and very rugged construction, it was harder to shoot down than the Japanese fighter. But it could not climb as quickly or turn as sharply.

A pilot with a great deal of combat experience might have been able to compensate for some of the Wildcat's shortcomings. But at this stage of the War, most U.S. Navy aviators had flown only 300 hours before assignment to a carrier and had never seen combat. Their enemy counterparts joined a ship after 700 hours in the cockpit, and the prowess of the Japanese pilots had steadily increased since their first operations off the coast of China in 1937.

Deficiencies in aircraft had haunted the U.S. Navy's fighter-squadron commanders for months before the outbreak of war. Among these concerned fliers was Lieutenant Commander John S. "Jimmy" Thach, leader of the *Saratoga's* Fighting 3. Studying intelligence reports of the

Zero's performance in China, which revealed its superior maneuverability, Thach decided that Wildcats, flying in the standard three-plane fighter section, would lose in a fight with the Zero. The tight, three-plane formation limited the defensive maneuverability of each Wildcat. After singling out an American fighter, a Zero pilot would almost certainly use his plane's sharper turn and faster climb to shoot down his foe.

Based at San Diego's North Island Naval Air Station during 1941 while the *Saratoga* was in port, Thach spent long hours arranging matchsticks in new formations on his dining-room table. One night he came up with an idea: a looser, four-plane formation composed of two sections that could weave back and forth across the sky to pick off attackers *(right)*.

Thach tried out the tactic in mock combat. "It was obvious from the beginning," he recalled, "that this maneuver was working even better than I had dreamed." Every time a plane attacked one of Thach's fighters, the aggressor faced the guns of another. In spite of successful demonstrations, the Navy was reluctant to embrace such a radical change. But later the technique was tried in actual combat and quickly proved itself. The Navy fully accepted the new tactic, which was appropriately christened the "Thach weave."

Trial in combat came early in 1942 for the American carrier pilots. In Washington the Chief of Naval Operations, Admiral Ernest J. King, decided to use his carriers to raid Japanese outposts in the Central Pacific. Such tactics would offer the least risk to his carriers—the only obstacle between the Japanese and Hawaii—and might slow the Japanese advance. With the *Saratoga* out of commission, some of her planes, including Thach's, were transferred to the *Lexington,* which, along with the *Enterprise* and the *Yorktown,* was primed for action.

In late January, Vice Admiral William F. Halsey Jr., an old sea dog who had come to carriers late in his career, sailed the *Enterprise* toward the Marshall Islands. On February 1, his Dauntless dive bombers attacked Japanese airfields at Roi and Taroa and sank a cargo ship and a submarine chaser at Kwajalein Atoll. Fighters from the Japanese bases slashed through the American formations, sometimes exhibiting peculiar behavior. After one pair of Japanese pilots bungled an attack against the dive bombers, Lieutenant Clarence Dickinson expected them to circle for another pass. Instead, he watched dumfounded as "out of range the two of them started doing stunts. They looped together and followed with an elegant slow roll. They had been sent to fight us but they just kept on waltzing in the sky." (It was not until after the War that the Americans learned the Japanese sometimes considered such stunts a necessity. "Usually we did acrobatics as signals," one Japanese pilot explained. "Our radios were so bad that often we had to signal by rolls, dives, wing overs.")

Between fighters and antiaircraft fire, the *Enterprise* lost 13 planes, and Halsey decided to withdraw that afternoon. The *Enterprise* had

Snaring Zeros with a deadly weave

"Fight as a team and you'll live longer," Lieutenant Commander J. S. "Jimmy" Thach told his men in 1942, after it became clear that the U.S. Navy's F4F Wildcat was no match for the Japanese Zero in single combat. Thach's solution was to fight in pairs—using the ingenious weaving tactic *(right)* he devised.

The F4Fs would fly parallel courses until attacked, then bank steeply inward. "The quick turn toward each other does two things to the enemy pilot," Thach explained. "It throws off his aim and, because he usually tries to follow his target, it leads him around into a position to be shot by the other part of our team." Convinced by the results, the Navy made the "Thach weave" standard practice and ordered its originator to teach the tactic to other fighter pilots.

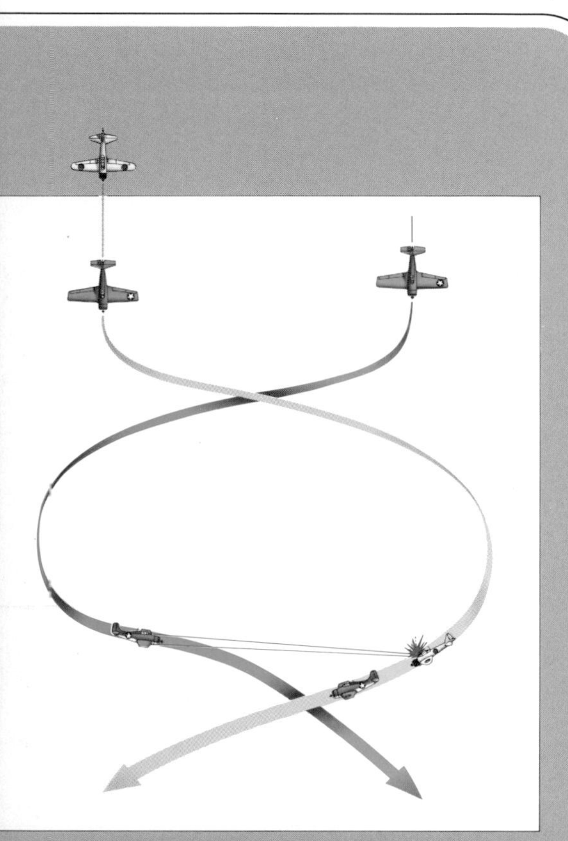

Two Wildcats side by side initiate a Thach weave as a Zero attacks from behind. Here, a kill is scored on the second turn.

Lieutenant Commander J. S. "Jimmy" Thach uses his hands to teach fighter tactics to new Navy pilots at Pearl Harbor in 1942. His maneuver was also adopted by the U.S. Army Air Forces, the British RAF and the Soviet Air Force.

been sailing within a small area for nine hours, a dangerously long time for a carrier to stay in one place if enemy planes were looking for her.

They were. About 1:30, five twin-engined Mitsubishi G4M Betty bombers slipped past the *Enterprise's* fighter cover and antiaircraft fire to aim 15 bombs at the carrier. All missed and, as the planes withdrew, patrolling Wildcats nailed the last plane in the formation, the "tail-end Charlie," as the Americans dubbed it. But instead of crashing into the sea, the pilot turned his crippled bomber around and headed straight for the carrier. As the ship's skipper, Captain George Murray, ordered the *Enterprise's* helmsman to turn hard to starboard to evade the plane, Aviation Machinist's Mate Second Class Bruno P. Gaido, an off-duty aerial gunner, raced across the deck toward a parked Dauntless dive bomber. He leaped into the rear seat, swung the machine gun mounted there toward the flaming Betty and let loose a stream of .30-caliber bullets at the rapidly approaching aircraft. Seconds later, the Betty's right wing clipped the rear of the Dauntless, shearing off the dive bomber's tail only three feet from Gaido, who stood up and kept firing as the Japanese plane flipped into the sea. He was promoted on the spot.

The War had come directly to the flattops. That morning, a few hundred miles south, the *Yorktown* and her escort of warships, commanded by Rear Admiral Frank Jack Fletcher, were stirring up trouble with the Japanese on Jaluit, Mili and Makin atolls by striking airfields and other military installations. At 1:07 p.m., Fletcher's radar picked up a bogey—Navy jargon for an unidentified aircraft—approaching the *Yorktown.* Fighter-director officers aboard the ship ordered two Wildcats, flown by Ensigns Scotty McCuskey and John Adams, to make the interception. Suddenly, the interloper broke out of the clouds 12 miles away, in full view of the ship. It was a Mavis, a Kawanishi H6K four-engined flying boat. For an anxious five seconds, all hands topside watched the Wildcats chase the Mavis into another cloud to the accompaniment of McCuskey's loud, radioed war whoops, which were broadcast over the *Yorktown's* loudspeakers. Then a few chunks of flaming wreckage fell from the clouds. After a moment's pause, McCuskey's voice rang out across the *Yorktown's* deck: "We just shot his ass off!" Amid cheers and laughter, the crippled bird plunged into the sea.

While the *Yorktown* and *Enterprise* fenced with the Japanese in the Marshalls, the *Lexington* embarked on a far more hazardous mission, penetrating deep into Japan's newly acquired waters in the Southwest Pacific for a surprise attack on Rabaul. With its fine harbor and airfields, Rabaul was a crucial advance base for the Japanese. As Japanese transport and supply ships poured troops and equipment into the port, scout planes fanned out 600 miles from Rabaul to find enemy vessels. The Japanese did not intend to be caught napping.

The Americans planned to attack on the morning of February 21. As the *Lexington* and her escort of warships approached Rabaul from the northeast, several SBD Dauntlesses scouted ahead to intercept and destroy any reconnaissance aircraft before they could report the advancing ships. But it was the *Lexington's* radar that detected a snooper at 10:15 a.m. on February 20, when the ship was still beyond striking distance of Rabaul. Captain Frederick C. "Ted" Sherman, skipper of the *Lexington*, ordered Jimmy Thach to intercept the plane.

Thach took off from the carrier with his wingman, and the two Wildcats climbed above the low-hanging, rain-spilling clouds to search for the source of the radar contact. Through gaps in the clouds, Thach spotted a Mavis cruising 5,000 feet below him. Alert to danger, the Japanese pilot scurried into a cloud bank and dived to escape. But the Wildcats were close behind and pounced on the flying boat when it broke through the overcast at 1,500 feet.

As the F4Fs attacked, tracers from the Mavis' turret cannon whizzed by. Once in range, the fighters opened fire with their machine guns. Thach punctured the Mavis' fuel tanks, but the plane sped on. Thach and his wingman circled for a second pass and this time found their mark. "Great white sheets of flame from the streaming fuel spread out behind him," said Thach, "and he began spinning down into the sea."

Aboard the *Lexington,* Sherman sounded general quarters, calling the crew to battle stations. The Mavis must surely have transmitted his position to Rabaul. Six fighters went up to relieve Thach's flight on patrol. Late in the afternoon Thach took off again with six Wildcats, but as the fighters he had relieved approached the *Lexington* to land, a formation of nine Japanese aircraft was detected by radar 76 miles away. Sherman ordered the returning Wildcats to rejoin Thach, whose section was already intercepting the planes—twin-engined bombers—at 11,000 feet. The Americans easily brought down five of the enemy aircraft, but four managed to drop their bombs, all of which missed the *Lexington.* As the planes withdrew, the fighters bagged two more; another fell to the *Lexington's* antiaircraft fire and one escaped.

At the height of the fracas, Sherman launched four fresh fighters, led by Lieutenant Edward "Butch" O'Hare. As they joined the battle, a second group of nine Japanese bombers approached. O'Hare and his wingman saw the raiders first and attacked. O'Hare fell in behind the Japanese and aimed at an engine of one bomber, watching in amazement as his bullets hit; the engine seemed to jump out of its wing mountings, and the plane dropped into the sea. O'Hare then shot an engine off the wing of a second bomber, and a third and a fourth.

All told, in just four minutes of action, O'Hare destroyed five of the bombers as the battle moved directly over the ships, their crews cheering wildly. O'Hare ran out of ammunition just as Jimmy Thach's flight, until now occupied with the first Japanese bomber formation, roared up to assist. But they were too late to prevent the four surviving Japanese planes from dropping their bombs. Fortunately the explosives detonated harmlessly as Captain Sherman adroitly swung the *Lexington* away from them. As the bombers turned for Rabaul, Thach's fighters got another chance at them and shot down three. The lone survivor, though damaged by the *Lexington's* gunners, escaped.

President Roosevelt congratulates Lieutenant Edward "Butch" O'Hare after awarding him the Medal of Honor in 1942 for downing five Japanese bombers. The ceremony was attended by (from left) Navy Secretary Frank Knox, Admiral Ernest J. King and the flier's wife.

With the element of surprise now lost, the American attack on Rabaul was canceled. Nevertheless, when the *Lexington* withdrew, the captain, the crew and the aviators could be very well pleased with themselves. Though two Wildcats had been lost in the action, only one pilot was killed; the other ditched alongside a destroyer and was rescued. Butch O'Hare, with five kills in one flight, had become the Navy's first ace of the War and was awarded the Medal of Honor.

Thach summed up the lesson of the battle. "It showed us," he said, "that the only real defense for a carrier or any other vessel against air attack is an airplane." The difficulty was that each carrier had a complement of only about 20 Wildcats, not enough of the sluggish fighters to repel a mass assault. More fighters would come, but only gradually as aircraft production was stepped up at home.

The wide-ranging forays of the U.S. carriers, which also attacked Salamaua and Lae in New Guinea, gave their crews and pilots invaluable combat experience. The attacks also bolstered morale, which had been low since Pearl Harbor. But they did not deter the Japanese, who proceeded with plans to take Port Moresby in New Guinea and Tulagi Island in the Solomons to extend eastward and southward their control of the Pacific. The presence of the American flattops, however, led the Japanese Army to insist on carrier support for these operations. Yamamoto hesitated to give it, preferring to mass his carrier forces in an effort to destroy the nettling American flattops once and for all. But in the end he agreed to lend his newest fleet carriers, the *Shokaku* and the *Zuikaku,* plus one light carrier, the *Shoho,* as additional air cover for Japan's assault forces. Destruction of the enemy carriers would have to wait until the Army could consolidate its pending conquests.

As details of these plans flashed between the various Japanese commands, they were overheard by U.S. listening posts and passed to cryptanalysts who were able to decipher some Japanese codes. From the fragments of messages that were decoded, Pacific Fleet intelligence specialists deduced the Japanese intentions. Thus Admiral Chester W. Nimitz, the Hawaii-based commander of the Pacific Fleet, knew by April 17 that three of Yamamoto's carriers would pass into the Coral Sea, south of the Solomon Islands, before the 3rd of May, en route to the action at Port Moresby and Tulagi. Time to prepare for the encounter was short. Fortunately the *Yorktown* was already on the scene and the *Lexington,* shipshape after a three-week sojourn at Pearl Harbor, was ready to join her. However, the *Enterprise* and *Hornet* were far away in the North Pacific on a special mission that could not affect the outcome of the War but that would be remembered for the boost it gave to American morale: On April 18, U.S. Army B-25s led by Lieutenant Colonel James H. Doolittle were launched from the deck of the *Hornet* in an audacious raid against the Japanese homeland. It was unlikely that the *Enterprise* and *Hornet* would have time to join the *Lexington* and *Yorktown* in challenging the Japanese invaders in the Coral Sea.

On May 3 Japanese forces protected by the *Shoho* occupied Tulagi. At dawn next day Fletcher, unaware of the *Shoho's* presence, launched a strike from the *Yorktown* against Tulagi. The American planes sank a destroyer, two patrol boats and a transport but never saw the *Shoho.* She had already left to join the ships en route to Port Moresby. The excited American pilots so wildly exaggerated their accomplishments that Fletcher believed, erroneously, that his planes had crushed the Tulagi force. So he shaped his course to join the *Lexington* for a confrontation with the Japanese carriers, leaving Tulagi to the enemy.

Fletcher's attack alerted the Japanese to the presence of the American carriers, and the *Shokaku* and *Zuikaku* under Admiral Takeo Takagi proceeded southward to engage the U.S. flattops. Fletcher, in overall command of the U.S. carriers, correctly deduced the Japanese avenue of approach. To bring matters to a head, he ordered the *Yorktown* and *Lexington* north to join battle, expecting to make contact on May 6. On that day the American and Japanese fleets were, in fact, within air-strike distance of each other, but neither realized it.

The problem was reconnaissance. Though each American carrier had a squadron of SBD dive bombers for scouting, Fletcher preferred to reserve most of his Dauntlesses to attack the enemy, not to scour the ocean in search of him. The Japanese on occasion used dive bombers and torpedo bombers as scouts, but the crews were not well trained in spotting ships from the air. Japanese flying boats, usually based far from the action, could rarely respond quickly to the carriers' tactical needs. Though neither Fletcher nor Takagi knew it, their flattops passed within 70 miles of each other during the night.

As the two fleets groped about the Coral Sea, American fighter pilots reviewed their tactics for the long-awaited contest between Zero and Wildcat. The battle would be a chance for the Thach weave to prove itself, though its inventor had been left in Hawaii to train green pilots.

Scouts from both fleets were airborne before dawn on May 7 and quickly made contact. At 7:30, a Japanese reconnaissance plane reported a carrier and a cruiser 200 miles south of the *Shokaku.* Putting Pearl Harbor veteran Lieutenant Commander Kakuichi Takahashi in charge of the mission, Admiral Takagi promptly launched a full deckload strike—as many planes as could fit on the flight deck—from both his carriers. The Battle of the Coral Sea was under way.

Warship recognition from high altitudes was and remains a difficult proposition, as Takahashi's fliers discovered when they attacked the two ships. The one reported as an aircraft carrier turned out to be the plump fleet oiler *Neosho,* which suffered bomb hits that would make it necessary to scuttle her several days later. Her consort, identified as a cruiser, was the destroyer *Sims,* which sank immediately after being struck by several bombs. Meanwhile, however, Takagi's scouts had sighted and correctly identified Fletcher's entire force.

Like Takagi, Fletcher began the battle with a mistaken idea of his foe's position. Early in the morning, when a *Yorktown* Dauntless reported two carriers and four cruisers 225 miles northwest, he sent off a deckload strike of 50 dive bombers, torpedo planes and fighters from the *Lexington.* Half an hour later, the *Yorktown* launched 43 planes toward the same target. Just then the scout that had reported the Japanese ships returned to the *Yorktown* and revealed that he had miscoded his report; he had actually sighted two cruisers and two destroyers. Thus Fletcher had not only apparently wasted a strike on comparatively minor Japanese ships, he also remained ignorant of Takagi's position.

But luck was to favor the Americans. At 11 a.m., Lieutenant Commander W. L. Hamilton, flying one of the *Lexington's* dive bombers toward the Japanese cruisers and destroyers, swept the dazzling ocean with binoculars from 15,000 feet and picked out "a number of thin white hairs on the blue sea." He radioed Lieutenant Commander Robert E. Dixon, leader of a flight of bomb-laden scouts 3,000 feet below. "Bob from Ham, enemy ships sighted 20 miles north." While Dixon strained to see, he passed the word to Lieutenant Commander Jimmy Brett of the Devastator torpedo planes flying several thousand feet

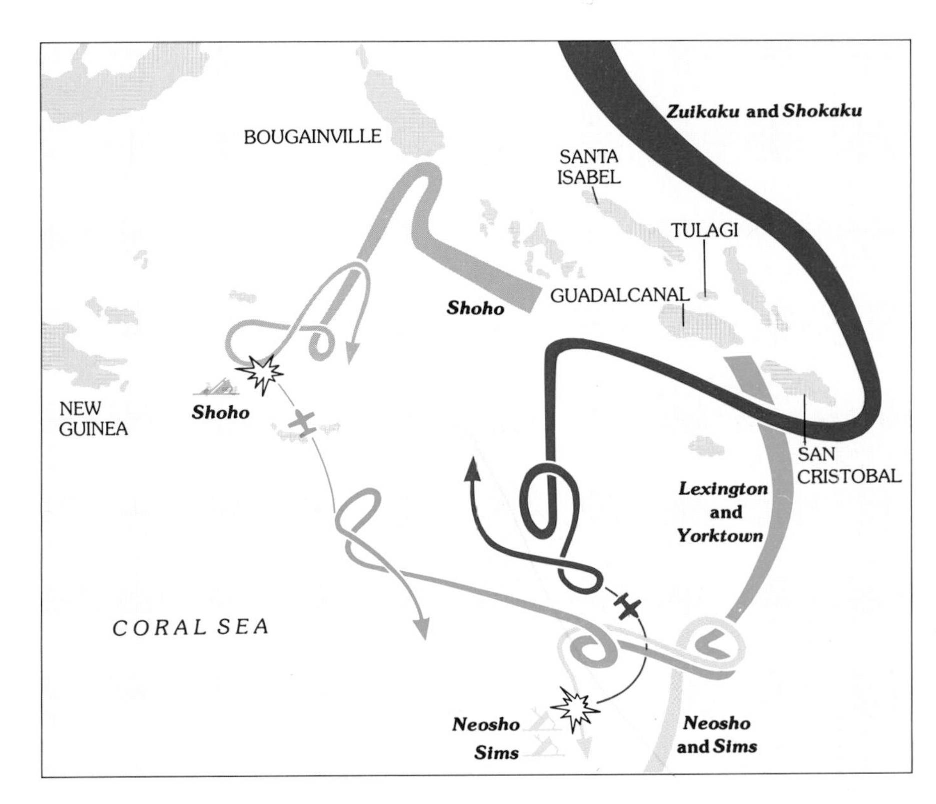

The Battle of the Coral Sea began early on May 7, 1942, when Japanese planes from the Shokaku and Zuikaku sank the U.S. oiler Neosho and destroyer Sims. Meanwhile, planes from the U.S. carriers Lexington and Yorktown, far to the west, sank the Japanese carrier Shoho, which was en route to attack New Guinea.

below him. Wildcats under Lieutenant Commander Paul Ramsey flew the customary top cover above 16,000 feet to ward off enemy fighters.

Turning toward the targets, Hamilton soon saw light reflecting off a flight deck. "I see one flattop bastard," he announced. It was the light carrier *Shoho:* Fletcher's strike would not be wasted after all. The SBDs dipped their noses into screeching dives, Dixon's squadron first. Hamilton waited to coordinate his dive-bombing runs with the masthead-level torpedo attacks by the TBDs. Fifteen minutes behind them came the flight from the *Yorktown.*

Lookouts on the *Shoho* first saw the attacking aircraft as they dropped below the cloud cover. The ship twisted and turned and the defending Zeros tried to stop the plummeting Dauntlesses—without success. It was difficult for a fighter to stop a dive bomber in a dive, since the fighter, lacking dive brakes, would speed past before it could do much shooting. Several bombs and torpedoes from both air groups struck the *Shoho,* starting a fire amid planes spotted on her deck for an attack that would never be launched.

Some 160 miles southeast of the action, anxious crewmen on the *Lexington* and *Yorktown* tried with little success to make sense of the many garbled radio transmissions from the scene of the battle. Then one message came through loud and clear: "Scratch one flattop! Dixon to carrier. Scratch one flattop!" The *Shoho* had gone down with 545 of her crew after a 30-minute battle; the cost had been only three American planes. Japanese invincibility seemed to be developing cracks, and Fletcher's airmen could now face the other enemy ships—if they could find them—with newfound confidence.

A torpedo from a U.S. Navy plane splashes into the sea (top), headed for the Japanese carrier Shoho on May 7, 1942. Hit by a total of 13 bombs and seven torpedoes, the Shoho burst into flames (bottom) and sank within five minutes, with a loss of more than 500 men.

For the moment, however, the Japanese had the advantage; they knew where to find the American carriers, and they set out to sink them. Their first attempt came that very day. When Commander Takahashi's planes returned after their attack on the *Neosho* and *Sims*, Admiral Takagi had them rearm, refuel and take off—15 Nakajima B5N torpedo planes and a dozen Aichi D3A dive bombers—for a late-afternoon strike. Since the planes would return after dark, no Zeros were launched; they were not equipped for flying at night.

Unfortunately for the Japanese, the raid went terribly awry. The U.S. carriers seemed to have evaporated. Takahashi's planes, finding nothing but rain, turned for home at sunset only to encounter four Wildcats led by Lieutenant Commander Ramsey. Lieutenant Commander Jimmy Flatley rushed in with reinforcements from the *Yorktown*. Without Zeros to protect them, Takahashi's bombers and torpedo planes were sitting ducks. Flatley bagged three, Ramsey two and the young pilots under their command got four more. Only two fighters were lost.

Takahashi's harried survivors regrouped and headed for their carriers—and flew right over the *Yorktown*. Mistaking the American ship for one of their own in the dark, some of the Japanese pilots lined up to land. "All hands, stand by to repel boarders," cried the *Yorktown's* gunnery officer, and the sailors opened fire. They shot down only one plane, but by the time the Japanese reached their own flattops 95 miles to the east, the pilots were exhausted. Eleven of them missed the flight deck as they tried to land in the dark and went into the drink. Only six, including Takahashi, survived the mission. To make matters worse, Admiral Takagi had lost the American carriers in the dark.

At dawn of May 8 Takagi launched reconnaissance aircraft to find them again. An hour later, Takahashi took off at the head of a strike force of 33 dive bombers and 18 torpedo planes escorted by 18 Zeros from the *Shokaku* and *Zuikaku*. If the American carriers were sighted, an air strike would already be aloft. Just minutes after Takahashi took off, Flight Warrant Officer Kenzo Kanno, scouting in a torpedo plane, sighted the U.S. carriers 200 miles south of the Japanese fleet. Kanno alerted his admiral, who relayed the news to Takahashi. Heading toward the American ships, Takahashi encountered the returning Kanno, who reversed course to show Takahashi the way—the supreme sacrifice, for Kanno now lacked enough fuel to return to his fleet.

Fletcher, too, had dispatched scouts at dawn. At 8:15 a.m. one of them radioed that he had seen two Japanese carriers 175 miles to the northeast. Shortly after 8:30 Fletcher launched a strike—39 planes from the *Yorktown* and 43 from the *Lexington*.

At 10:30 the *Yorktown's* strike sighted the two Japanese carriers through a lucky break in the clouds; they were the *Zuikaku* and the *Shokaku*. Zeros rose to meet the threat. As the *Zuikaku* scurried into a rain squall for cover, the Devastators swept in low against the *Shokaku*. Though the planes, effectively protected by their escort of Wildcats, managed to launch their torpedoes, many of the slow-running missiles were evaded by the turning carrier and the few that struck the ship failed to detonate. As the Devastators roared away through the *Shokaku's* frenzied antiaircraft fire, seven Dauntlesses of the *Yorktown's* Scouting 5 dived on the carrier from 17,000 feet through a pack of two dozen Zeros. Their bombs all missed, but those of the *Yorktown's* Bombing 5, following close behind, did not. Lieutenant John J. Powers plunged his Dauntless dive bomber through the Japanese defenses. Though wounded, he kept diving, releasing his 1,000-pound bomb from an altitude of only 200 feet and planting it squarely on the *Shokaku's* flight deck. He crashed into the sea next to his target; his courage earned him a posthumous Medal of Honor. Then a second bomb found the mark, and flames billowed from the forward part of the carrier's flight deck.

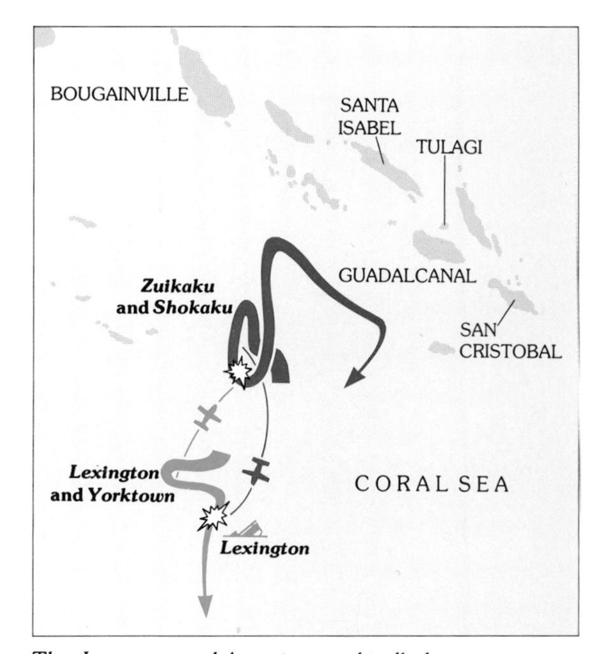

The Japanese and Americans rekindled the Battle of the Coral Sea on May 8 with simultaneous strikes against each other's carriers. Planes from the Zuikaku and Shokaku severely damaged the Lexington—she sank in the evening—and battered the Yorktown, which withdrew southward. American dive bombers, unable to find the Zuikaku, managed to hit the Shokaku but could not sink her.

Damage crews on the Lexington struggle to put out fires after the ship was struck by Japanese bombs and torpedoes in the Battle of the Coral Sea. When it became obvious that the carrier could not be saved, destroyers drew alongside to take on the wounded and all hands prepared for evacuation (overleaf).

Because of thick clouds, some of the *Lexington's* planes never found the enemy fleet. One that did scored with another bomb on the *Shokaku,* as a swarm of Zeros ripped into the four-plane fighter escort led by Lieutenant Noel Gayler. "There was always one of them making a run at me," said Gayler. "Early in the scrap I evaded the attack of one and then jumped his tail. He immediately resorted to the old Zero trick of zooming for altitude. I anticipated the pull-up and gave him a snap burst as he commenced his climb. My bullets hit him and he began to burn." Gayler ducked into a cloud, then sneaked out and blasted another Zero. But the sky was so cloudy that the Wildcat pilots often could not see one another. Under such conditions the Thach weave was useless, and Gayler's three mates were soon shot down. Gayler, seeing the *Shokaku* in flames, headed back to the *Lexington.* By noon the battle swirling above the burning *Shokaku* had ended, and she radioed her fighters to land on the *Zuikaku* when that carrier emerged from the squall.

Meanwhile, at 10:55, the *Lexington's* radar picked up the approaching Japanese strike. Only eight fighters were available to meet the 69 attackers. At 11:18 three Kates launched torpedoes at the *Yorktown.* Taking advantage of the ship's agility, Captain Elliott Buckmaster swung her out of danger. Altogether, eight torpedoes were aimed at the ship and Buckmaster managed to dodge all of them, as well as most of the bombs from Val dive bombers. Most, but not all. One plunged through the flight deck and detonated four decks below, killing or injuring 66 men. Fires erupted but were rapidly brought under control, and flight operations were not interrupted.

A mile away, the *Lexington* was having a rougher time. Simulta-

Crewmen of the burning U.S. carrier Lexington clamber over the side on ropes after receiving the order to abandon ship.

neously with the first torpedo attack on the *Yorktown,* Commander Shimazaki, who had led the second wave at Pearl Harbor, flew toward the *Lexington* and into a "virtual wall of antiaircraft fire," as he described it shortly after the battle. "It seemed impossible that we could survive our bombing and torpedo runs through such incredible defenses. Burning and shattered planes of both sides plunged from the skies." Amid "this fantastic 'rainfall' of antiaircraft and spinning planes," he dived almost to the water's surface and released his torpedo. As Shimazaki pulled up, he "could see the crewmen on the ship staring at my plane as it rushed by."

The *Lexington* turned more slowly than the *Yorktown.* Consequently, Captain Sherman could not steer clear of all 11 torpedoes launched almost at once against both sides of his ship. Two struck home. Within seconds, dive-bombing Vals registered two hits; one detonated a box of 5-inch antiaircraft shells and the other damaged the smokestack. Water rushing through the gaping holes blasted in the *Lexington's* hull by torpedoes gave the ship a 7-degree list. Boiler rooms were awash, and the aircraft elevators were out of commission. Nonetheless, the *Lexington* resumed flight operations less than an hour after the last Japanese marauder had disappeared over the horizon. But just when Sherman was certain that the damage was under control, the situation abruptly changed. Aviation-fuel vapors in the bowels of the ship were ignited by a sparking generator. Explosion followed explosion with increasing violence. Reluctantly, Sherman ordered the ship abandoned shortly after 5 p.m. By then 216 crewmen had died, but the remaining 2,735 were rescued and 19 aircraft were transferred to the *Yorktown.* In the evening, the *Lexington* was scuttled by torpedoes from the destroyer *Phelps,* a sad occasion for the carrier's crew, watching from rescue vessels. Said Seaman Herbert Lentz, a gunner aboard the *Lexington,* "All the fellows were crying and weeping like young girls, so was I."

On the basis of ships sunk, the Japanese won the Battle of the Coral Sea, the first fleet engagement in which aircraft were responsible for all the destruction that occurred. In payment for the *Lexington,* the oiler *Neosho* and the destroyer *Sims,* Admiral Takagi had lost only the *Shoho*—a small carrier compared with the *Lexington*—and a handful of minor ships at Tulagi. Though the *Shokaku* seemed to have been badly damaged, she made it to port under her own steam. Two months later she would be repaired and ready for action. The *Zuikaku,* unscarred in the battle, was out of action for little more than a month while she replaced the planes and crews that had been shot down.

But ships tell only part of the tale. The Americans could claim a victory in the Coral Sea despite their losses, because Fletcher's carriers had stopped the Japanese in their tracks. Before midnight on May 7, as the battle was shaping up, Admiral Shigeyoshi Inoue at Rabaul, in charge of the Port Moresby invasion, had ordered the operation postponed until the U.S. carriers could be driven off. The operation would never resume. Japan's aura of invincibility had been shattered.

The aerial match-up

Before Pearl Harbor, many military experts believed that Japanese warplanes were, at best, only second-rate copies of Western models. "The ability to produce original designs is lacking," said a U.S. military attaché in a secret report from Tokyo in 1938. The fact is that Japanese aircraft designers had developed modern naval fighters, torpedo planes and dive bombers that rivaled American carrier aircraft and in some cases were clearly superior; the first months of the War brought a series of stunning surprises to American air experts.

The American and Japanese carrier planes that opened the War are presented in pairs here and on the following pages. The dates these particular models entered service are noted, and the paired aircraft are reproduced in scale to each other.

Numerically, at least, the Japanese and the Americans began the War evenly matched, with roughly 500 carrier-based planes each. But Japan's lightly built machines were, in general, more maneuverable and possessed greater speed and range than the American planes. These advantages came at a price: In order to save weight, Japanese designers had sacrificed certain items, such as armor plate and self-sealing fuel tanks, that the Americans considered essential. As a rule, U.S. Navy planes were not only less vulnerable but also had greater firepower.

At first the Americans had difficulty identifying the various Japanese planes, each of which had several designations based on different systems. One was a letter and numeral code similar to that of the U.S. Navy; another was a type number derived from the last digits of the year in which the plane was approved for production, as numbered by the ancient Japanese calendar. Thus the famous Mitsubishi A6M2 carrier fighter was also known as the Zero because it was approved in the Japanese calendar year 2600 (1940). Eventually, the Allies devised their own code names for Japanese airplanes, assigning male names to fighters and female names to bombers, transports and flying boats.

NAKAJIMA B5N2 TYPE 97 CARRIER ATTACK BOMBER (1940)
Code-named Kate by the Allies, the B5N2 was—despite its designation as a bomber—the best torpedo plane in the world in 1941. It had a top speed of 235 mph and could carry a 1,764-pound payload.

DOUGLAS TBD-1 DEVASTATOR TORPEDO BOMBER (1937)
The U.S. Navy's first all-metal, low-wing aircraft, the Devastator was obsolete by the outbreak of war. Its maximum speed of 206 mph and cruising speed of only 128 made it easy prey. It carried a half-ton torpedo.

A murderous pair of dive bombers

The U.S. Navy's Douglas SBD-3 Dauntless dive bomber was one of the few American carrier planes not inferior in performance to their Japanese counterparts at the outbreak of war. The Dauntless had a longer range, could carry a greater payload and was somewhat faster than the Aichi D3A1 bomber, which was code-named Val by the Allies and was considered obsolescent in 1941.

Even so, Vals sank more Allied fighting ships during the War than any other type of Axis aircraft, starting at Pearl Harbor, where Vals took a heavy toll on the American warships and airfields. Six months later the Americans got a chance to even the score at the crucial Battle of Midway—where the Dauntless became famous as the plane that helped alter the course of the Pacific war.

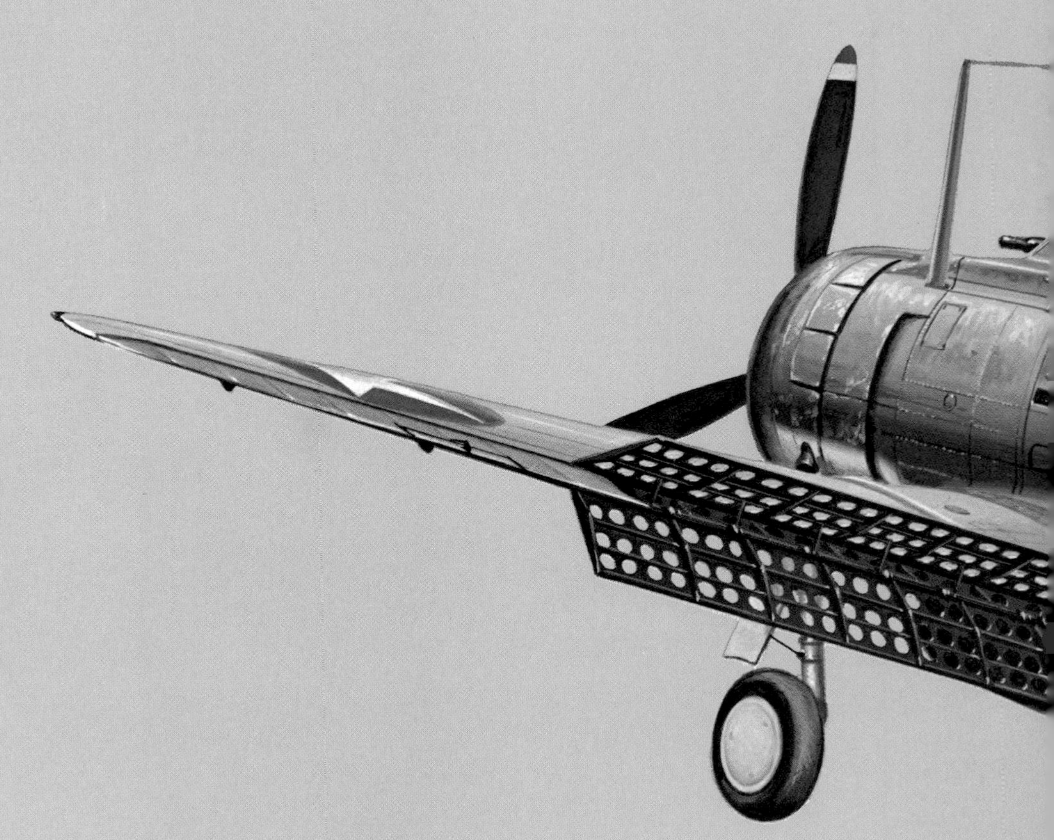

AICHI D3A1 TYPE 99 CARRIER BOMBER (1940)
With fixed landing gear, the Val had a top speed of only 240 mph. But this dive bomber was so maneuverable that it was also used as a fighter. It could carry a 551-pound bomb under the fuselage and two 132-pound bombs on underwing racks.

DOUGLAS SBD-3 DAUNTLESS DIVE BOMBER (1941)
One of the great carrier planes of all time, this rugged dive bomber, with a maximum speed of 250 mph, was only slightly faster than the Val but carried 1,200 pounds of bombs. This one, shown with its dive brakes open, flew from the Enterprise.

Rivals for command of the Pacific skies

At the outbreak of war, the U.S. Navy had nothing in its arsenal to match the superb Mitsubishi A6M2 carrier fighter—code-named Zeke by the Allies but universally known as the Zero. The stubby Grumman F4F Wildcat was the standard American carrier fighter until 1943, and, though extremely rugged, it did not have the speed, maneuverability or range to meet the Zero on equal terms.

The Americans quickly learned to rely on team tactics whenever they encountered the nimble Zero. Even so, it was not until later in the War, when faster and more modern American fighters began to appear in large numbers, that the Americans were finally able to wrest command of the air from the pilots of the Imperial Japanese Navy.

MITSUBISHI A6M2 TYPE O CARRIER FIGHTER (1940)
Although its engine produced only 950 hp, the lightly built Zero could fly about 330 mph and had a range of 1,930 miles with its belly drop tank. It had two 7.7-mm. machine guns and two 20-mm. cannon. Lieutenant Commander Shigeru Itaya led the first wave of fighters from the carrier Akagi to Pearl Harbor in 1941 in this one.

GRUMMAN F4F-4 WILDCAT CARRIER FIGHTER (1942)
Armed with six .50-caliber machine guns, the Wildcat had self-sealing fuel tanks, protective armor plate and a 1,200-hp engine, but it was sluggish compared with the Zero and had a range of only 770 miles.

3

Turning point at Midway

The Battle of the Coral Sea may have been a standoff, but to Japan the disappointing outcome did not appear to be of critical importance. Although the seizure of Port Moresby might have to be postponed, Japan had no intention of abandoning that goal or any other objective necessary to victory. Indeed, Admiral Yamamoto had a plan that he was certain would lure the enemy's aircraft carriers to their doom and end American hopes of winning the war in the Pacific. Yamamoto would attack Midway.

Midway lies 1,150 miles west-northwest of Oahu. Yamamoto judged that his adversary Admiral Nimitz would be unwilling to tolerate a Japanese base so uncomfortably close to Pearl Harbor; Nimitz would have to rush his carriers to Midway, and there Yamamoto would annihilate them with an armada of unprecedented strength. A new battleship named the *Yamato*—at more than 70,000 tons, the largest ever built—would make her debut as the flagship of a fleet of four large aircraft carriers, 11 battleships and some 200 other vessels, including cruisers, destroyers, oilers and troopships carrying an assault force of 5,000 men.

Yamamoto's scheme was a complex one. First, a diversionary force would attack the Aleutian Islands in the North Pacific to draw the U.S. Pacific Fleet away from Midway. The next day Japanese carrier aircraft would strike at Midway, and the day after that ground forces would surge ashore to capture the airfield there. Meanwhile, the Americans would certainly abandon the Aleutians to rescue Midway. But by the time they reached the island—four days after the first shots were fired, Yamamoto reckoned—Midway would be securely in Japanese hands, and he could turn his full attention to sinking the American carriers. Any ships that escaped Japanese aircraft would be mopped up by battleships and cruisers held in reserve.

Yamamoto had decided to proceed without waiting for the *Shokaku* to be repaired and the *Zuikaku* to be replenished with new aircraft and new aviators. He considered his force more than ample to handle the *Enterprise* and the *Hornet,* the only U.S. carriers that the Japanese thought were fit for duty in the Pacific after the Battle of the Coral Sea.

Pilots of the Hornet's Torpedo Squadron 8 gather for a 1942 group portrait taken shortly before all but one of them—Ensign George Gay (kneeling, center)—were killed in the Battle of Midway.

As sound as Yamamoto's plan appeared to be, it had a fundamental weakness: The success of the entire operation depended on Admiral Nimitz' reacting precisely as the Japanese predicted, which in turn depended on the details of the plan being kept secret. But thanks to the U.S. Navy's codebreakers, Admiral Nimitz could scarcely have been better informed about Japanese intentions had he sat at Yamamoto's side. By the middle of May he knew of his adversary's general intentions, and before the end of the month his intelligence staff had deduced its specifics, including the diversionary move against the Aleutians and the time Yamamoto had set for the air strikes against Midway: 6:00 a.m. on June 4.

With these facts in hand, Nimitz immediately began assembling his forces. Admiral Halsey's Task Force 16, which included the aircraft carriers *Enterprise* and *Hornet,* was in the South Pacific, where it had arrived too late for the Battle of the Coral Sea. Halsey was now ordered to take his ships to Pearl Harbor and prepare for the coming clash with the Japanese; meanwhile, phony radio messages led the Japanese to believe that the *Hornet* and *Enterprise* remained in the south. The *Yorktown* also made for Pearl, where the shipyard—in a Herculean effort that lasted two days and two nights—patched her up for the approaching battle. While in Hawaii, the carriers traded in their old Wildcats for a newer version with folding wings that allowed more fighters to be squeezed aboard.

Nimitz thus had three large carriers and greatly increased fighter protection with which to face Yamamoto's four flattops, but these odds were still not enough to assure an American victory. To make matters worse, Nimitz' most experienced carrier commander would miss the action: Halsey had been hospitalized with dermatitis brought on by overwork. To lead the *Enterprise* and *Hornet* task force in his stead, Nimitz, on Halsey's advice, selected Rear Admiral Raymond A. Spruance, who had commanded the screen of warships that guarded Halsey's carriers. Spruance had no experience in carrier command, but the expert staff that he inherited would help compensate for that deficiency. Rear Admiral Frank Jack Fletcher would lead the *Yorktown* task force and, as senior officer afloat, would direct the battle. There were some command shifts at lower levels as well. One was the appointment of Lieutenant Commander Jimmy Thach to take over the *Yorktown's* fighters from Jimmy Flatley, who returned to the States to train a new fighter squadron.

Many of the American pilots had never seen combat. Even Commander John C. Waldron, leader of the *Hornet's* Torpedo Squadron 8 and, at 41, the oldest squadron commander on any of the carriers, was uninitiated, but he knew what to do. "Attack," was his unit's motto, and its emblem was a clenched fist. During the preceding autumn Waldron had drilled his young pilots mercilessly. By day, he had them spend six to eight hours in the cockpit; at night, he lectured to them from his bible of torpedo bombing, a manual of tactics he himself had written.

Admiral Chester W. Nimitz, the mastermind of the American forces at Midway, gazes pensively out the window of a Navy plane in 1942. Nimitz' quiet mien made him a father figure to his men: "His smile and his blue eyes would go right through you," said one.

For all of their enthusiasm, however, the torpedo pilots were hamstrung by the lackluster performance of their aircraft, the Douglas TBD Devastator, whose cruising speed of 128 miles per hour made it an easy target for the enemy. So little confidence did the TBD inspire that Ensign William W. Abercrombie, one of Waldron's pilots, dubbed Torpedo 8 the Coffin Squadron. Hope lay in the replacement for the TBD—the new Grumman TBF Avenger. Nineteen of these aircraft, flown by a detachment of Torpedo 8 pilots, arrived in Hawaii—but a day after the *Hornet* had sailed; she would have to meet the Japanese without them. Not all of them would miss the battle, however; six of the TBFs—and only six—were flown to Midway under Lieutenant Langdon K. Fieberling.

When they landed on Midway, it became clear why so few of the TBFs had been ordered there. The airfield was too crowded to accommodate more. Admiral Nimitz was packing Midway with planes to search out and attack the Japanese fleet in concert with his carrier aircraft. Besides the six TBFs, there were 32 PBY Catalina flying boats, 19 Army B-17 and four B-26 bombers, and a hodgepodge of Marine Corps aircraft: 20 old F2A Buffalo fighters, 16 SBDs, 11 obsolete SB2U Vindicator dive bombers, and six Wildcats.

Admiral Spruance had left Pearl Harbor with the *Enterprise* and *Hornet* and the rest of Task Force 16 on May 28, followed two days later by Admiral Fletcher in the *Yorktown,* flagship of Task Force 17. The two groups rendezvoused northeast of Midway on June 2 and sent up search planes to supplement reconnaissance by the Catalinas from Midway. Nimitz also had 25 submarines deployed looking for the Japanese fleet, which, according to intelligence reports, was to have sailed from Japan late in May.

As expected, Vice Admiral Chuichi Nagumo, commander of the Japanese Carrier Strike Force, had left home waters on May 26 with the *Akagi, Kaga, Hiryu* and *Soryu.* His course across the Pacific followed a front of heavy weather that provided effective cover from American search planes. But Nagumo was hampered by the illness of several key officers. Commander Minoru Genda, the force's tactician, was laid low with fever. Commander Mitsuo Fuchida, who was to have led the air strikes against Midway and the enemy carriers, had been incapacitated by an emergency appendectomy. And Yamamoto, aboard his flagship, the *Yamato,* was suffering from severe stomach cramps caused by a parasitical disease.

Even more vexing was a dearth of information about the American carriers. Plans for aerial reconnaissance of Pearl Harbor had been foiled when several U.S. Navy vessels anchored at the very spot where Kawanishi H8K flying boats were to refuel from submarines on their way to Hawaii. Moreover, radio traffic indicated that the United States forces had increased long-range air searches. The Americans clearly knew something was afoot.

The Japanese battle plan anticipated that the U.S. flattops would not appear at Midway before June 7. By then, the island would be securely under Japanese control and Nagumo could break his four carriers out of Genda's box formation—intended for pounding targets ashore—and into an arrangement that was looser and safer for a battle between ships. If, however, the U.S. carriers were to arrive before Midway had been taken, Nagumo would have to divide his attention between land and sea engagements and fight one or the other from an unsuitable formation. By contrast, the U.S. carriers would have only one concern—Nagumo.

On the morning of June 3, a Catalina discovered some of the Japanese transports that were carrying troops to Midway. Within hours, they were attacked by nine Midway-based B-17s, but all the bombs missed. Soon after, word arrived that Japanese carrier planes—from the *Ryujo* and *Junyo*—had attacked Dutch Harbor in the Aleutians.

The American commanders refused to bite at the Aleutian lure, knowing it to be a diversion. Instead, Admirals Fletcher and Spruance headed for waters north of Midway, where they expected to intercept Nagumo's four flattops the next morning.

The atmosphere in the pilots' ready rooms on all three American carriers was tense that night. The torpedo-plane pilots were especially concerned. Lieutenant Commander Lance Massey on board the *Yorktown* doubted whether his Torpedo Squadron 3 could survive the antiaircraft fire from a well-defended fleet. On the *Hornet,* Jack Waldron told Torpedo 8, "The approaching battle will be the biggest of the War and may well be the turning point also." He explained that they would make their first attack in the early morning and fly as many strikes as possible throughout the day—including one attack after nightfall. A final word of advice betrayed Waldron's inner concern: The airmen should write letters to their families, he counseled, "just in case some of us don't get back."

Half an hour before sunrise on June 4, 1942, Admiral Fletcher launched 10 scouts from the *Yorktown.* But it was a Catalina from Midway that first sighted two Japanese carriers some 200 miles west-southwest of Spruance's Task Force 16. A flight of more than 100 enemy carrier planes was already en route to the island. Radar picked them up when they were 93 miles away, and all planes on Midway were in the air before the intruders arrived. The PBYs were ordered to keep clear; the six TBFs of Lieutenant Fieberling's Torpedo 8 detachment plus four Army B-26s armed with torpedoes were to go after the enemy carriers immediately; the Army's B-17 bombers and Marine Dauntless and Vindicator dive bombers were to follow them; and the Marine fighters were sent to intercept the raiders.

At 6:16 a.m., only minutes after the last plane had left Midway, a Marine pilot shouted "Tallyho!" into his radio and the fighters swooped down onto the enemy formation. The Marines were bludgeoned. Of the 27 Buffalos and Wildcats, 17 were shot down and seven badly damaged. Even so, the Marines scored some kills, and antiaircraft

Dauntless pilots dived with their canopies open for easy escape, falling on the enemy at a 75-degree angle that gave defending gunners little time to find their mark.

Dive bombing: a nerve-racking art

Both sides in the Pacific war relied on dive bombing to hit elusive targets at sea, but this sort of attack, which was inherently more accurate than level bombing, required a high degree of flying skill.

A dive-bomber pilot staked out his prey from as high as 12,000 feet. He opened dive flaps to limit his speed, retarded the throttle, then half-rolled into a nearly vertical plunge lasting 35 to 40 brutal seconds. As he plummeted through the enemy's umbrella of antiaircraft fire, he plied his ailerons to adjust for the wind and the movement of his target. At 2,000 to 1,500 feet, he loosed a single bomb and then wrenched the plane's nose up. As the aircraft banked away, the pilot was subjected to heavy centrifugal pressure—typically five to six times the force of gravity.

The delivery was hair-raising, but it made the bombs pay. Off Midway, U.S. Navy dive bombers put four enemy flattops beneath 2,000 fathoms of sea.

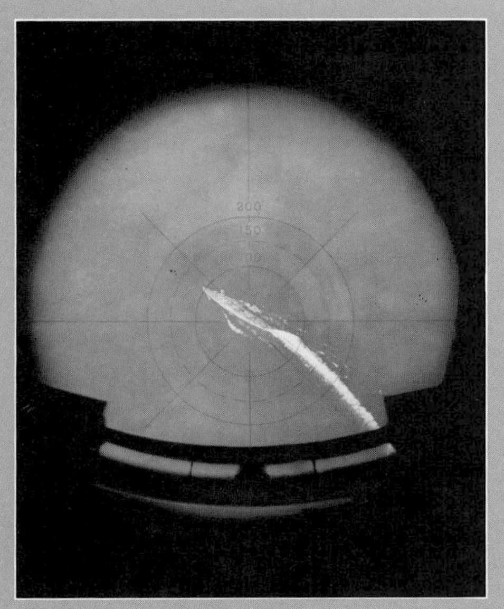

A destroyer is bracketed by the cross hairs of a dive-bombing sight. A bubble at the bottom of the lens indicates that the plane is not slipping to one side.

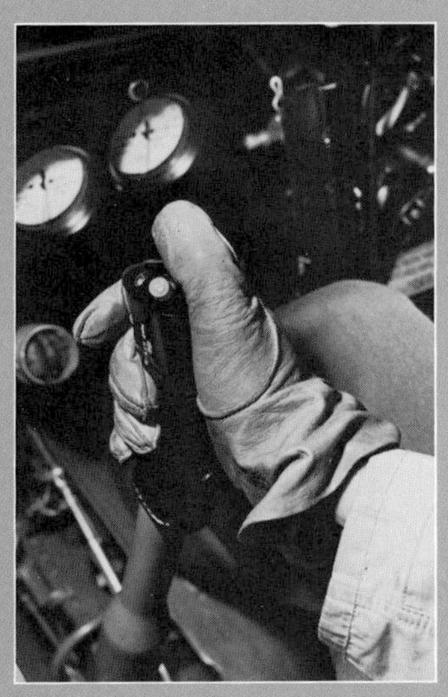

A pilot's thumb is poised over the bomb-release button, set in the head of the plane's control stick. The pilot triggered machine guns with a button on the front of the stick.

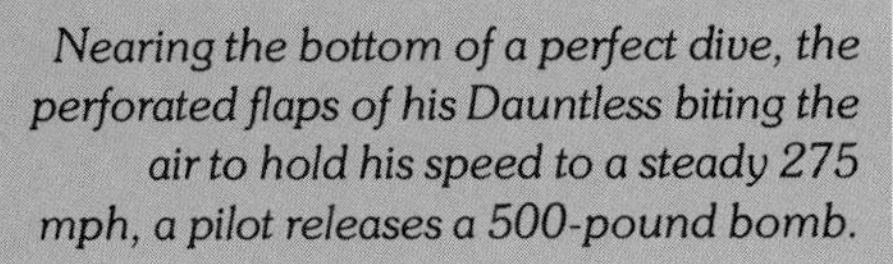

Nearing the bottom of a perfect dive, the perforated flaps of his Dauntless biting the air to hold his speed to a steady 275 mph, a pilot releases a 500-pound bomb.

fire from Midway's guns knocked one third of the attackers from the sky.

As the melee erupted over Midway, the U.S. admirals at sea had to decide how to attack the Japanese carriers. Fletcher could not immediately launch a strike from the *Yorktown;* his scouts, returning to the ship low on fuel, had to be taken aboard before the flight deck could be rearranged for launching aircraft. So at 6:07 he ordered Spruance on the *Enterprise* to attack first.

Spruance had planned to steam for three more hours, shortening the distance between his and Nagumo's carriers to less than 100 miles. But his staff intervened. "Our one and combined thought," operations officer Commander William H. Buracker would recall, "was to hit as soon as we could." The chief of staff, Captain Miles Browning, pointed out to Spruance that if they launched two hours earlier, at 7:00 instead of 9:00, the strike might well reach the enemy carriers at their most vulnerable moment, when Japanese aircraft returning from Midway would be refueling and rearming. Aviation fuel, bombs and torpedoes exposed on the flight decks would make the Japanese carriers floating tinderboxes. Spruance recognized sound advice when he heard it. Even though the TBDs and their escorting fighters would be stretched beyond their maximum range and might not make it back to the carriers, he approved Browning's recommendation and ordered the call to flight quarters.

Amid last-minute preparations, Lieutenant Raymond A. Moore, usually a quiet fellow, teased Ensign George Gay of Torpedo 8. "You'll never get a hit, Gay," Moore taunted. "You couldn't hit a bull in the tail with a six-foot rake." Gay was in no mood for jokes. "I'll get a hit," he replied grimly as the pilots filed to their planes.

Admiral Spruance had decided to strike with every bit of strength he could muster. All 15 of the *Hornet's* TBD Devastators were tapped for the mission. So were 35 SBD Dauntlesses of Scouting 8 and Bombing 8, escorted by 10 fighters. From the *Enterprise,* air-group leader Lieutenant Commander Clarence Wade McClusky would lead a strike group of 32 SBDs from Bombing 6 and Scouting 6. Lieutenant Commander Eugene Lindsey took all 14 TBDs of Torpedo 6, and Fighting 6 provided 10 Wildcats. In all, 116 aircraft were to descend on the enemy carriers, leaving 36 fighters and eight SBDs to protect Task Force 16 from Japanese aircraft and submarines. The *Hornet* and the *Enterprise* turned away from each other and took up stations several miles apart to launch their strikes—the same tactic preached by Genda for the Japanese fleet.

In the meantime, Nagumo, unaware that American carriers were in the area, still had his flattops bunched together to attack Midway. As a precaution, however, he sent out seven scouts and ordered the arming of 108 bombers, fighters and torpedo planes just in case an enemy surface force was sighted. Two of the scout planes, from the heavy cruiser *Tone,* were launched half an hour late because of catapult problems. The delay was to prove a costly one.

At 7:00, just as Spruance launched the first of his strike aircraft, Nagumo received a radio message from Lieutenant Joichi Tomonaga, leader of the attack on Midway. Tomonaga reported that a second strike was necessary to complete the destruction of Midway's defenses. Before Nagumo and his staff could act on this information, a destroyer in his screen signaled that a flight of enemy planes was approaching. They were the four torpedo-bearing B-26s and Lieutenant Fieberling's TBF detachment of Torpedo 8 from Midway. They had been sent out without a fighter escort so that Midway's fighters could defend the island.

Fieberling kept the TBFs just under the clouds, at 4,000 feet, until they spotted the Japanese fleet at 7:10. Almost simultaneously, Zeros swarmed in. "Here they come!" shouted Jay Manning, turret gunner in a TBF flown by Ensign Bert Earnest, as more than two dozen Zeros dropped out of the clouds, 20-millimeter cannon spurting. Manning replied with his .50-caliber machine gun for a few seconds, then a shell slammed into his chest. Radioman Harry Ferrier at the .30-caliber machine gun mounted under the plane's belly looked up at his pal. "The sight of his slumped and lifeless body startled me. Quite suddenly, I was a scared, mature old man at 18. I had never seen death before. I lost all sense of time and direction but huddled by my gun hoping for a chance to shoot back."

He did not get it. As the six unescorted torpedo planes descended at full throttle, making for the *Akagi,* round after round ripped into them. Bullets bounced off the armor plate behind each pilot. One shell punctured a hydraulic line in Earnest's aircraft, and the tail wheel swung down out of its well to block Ferrier's gun. One slug grazed Earnest's jaw, and others nicked Ferrier in the wrist and head, briefly knocking him unconscious. Earnest opened his bomb-bay doors as his much-holed Avenger passed over the outer ring of ships protecting the *Akagi,* but another shell damaged the plane's controls, and it descended closer to the water. "I veered out of the formation," Earnest recalled, "and tried to control my altitude with my rudder and ailerons, but it didn't work. I thought I was all through, so I aimed my torpedo as best I could at the nearest ship, a four-stacker light cruiser, and dropped." Then he managed to regain altitude and headed away from the enemy fleet, two Zeros on his tail.

"I tried everything I had ever heard of to avoid their fire," he said. "I sideslipped, I chopped the throttle, I turned and twisted and jinked. Finally they ran out of ammunition and left me." His electric compass shot to bits, Earnest navigated by the sun until he saw a pall of smoke. It was Midway. With only one wheel down, he made a crash landing that both he and Ferrier survived. Two of the B-26s also limped back to Midway, but the rest of the aircraft failed to return. Not a single torpedo had scored.

As the American planes dropped from the sky around him, Admiral Nagumo correctly deduced that they had come from Midway and agreed with Tomonaga that the island needed a second attack. At

7:15, he set the process in motion: The torpedo bombers that had been standing by on the *Kaga* and *Akagi* in case an enemy carrier showed up were moved belowdecks so that their torpedoes and armor-piercing bombs could be exchanged for general-purpose bombs to use against Midway. This decision was a gamble, but no American ships had been reported and none were expected. Arming crews raced feverishly to switch the ordnance.

Only 13 minutes later, the situation changed radically. One of the scout planes that had taken off late from the *Tone* reported sighting "10 ships, probably enemy" 200 miles to the east of Nagumo. Had the scout taken off on time and the report come half an hour sooner, Nagumo would have had 36 torpedo-armed planes ready to strike. As it was, some of those aircraft were already back on the flight decks, loaded with bombs meant for land targets, and the rest were still below. At 7:45 he ordered a temporary halt to the weapons switch.

Before he could decide on his next move, he found himself under attack again. Sixteen Marine Corps SBD dive bombers appeared from Midway. Zeros tore into this force, destroying half and repulsing the others. Hard on their heels followed 15 B-17s, then 11 Vindicator dive bombers, none of which scored better than near misses. At the height of this assault, the Japanese scout from the *Tone* updated his report: The force of 10 U.S. surface ships he was shadowing was "accompanied by what appears to be an aircraft carrier." Nagumo's deci-

Penetrating heavy defensive fire, a Devastator flown by Ensign George "Tex" Gay delivers its torpedo in this painting of the assault on the Japanese carrier Kaga. Gay then ditched his crippled plane and he floated helplessly amid the Japanese fleet until he was rescued by a seaplane.

Ensign Gay and his nurse at a Pearl Harbor hospital soak up the delirious news accounts of the Battle of Midway. As the only surviving member of Torpedo Squadron 8, the ensign was an instant celebrity, and Admiral Nimitz kept the flier front and center for the press.

sion had been made for him. He ordered the torpedo planes on deck rearmed with their original ordnance—torpedoes and armor-piercing bombs. The weary ordnance teams set to work again, removing the general-purpose bombs and stowing them about the hangar decks to save precious minutes.

Although all the American air attacks had failed abjectly, the Japanese battle plan was beginning to fray at the edges. Midway had not yet been battered enough for Yamamoto's amphibious forces to storm ashore. Air attacks launched from the island had forced Nagumo's ships into evasive maneuvers that threatened the integrity of the box formation. Moreover, at least one American aircraft carrier was on the scene three days earlier than expected.

Japanese doctrine dictated that, with an enemy flattop within striking distance, Nagumo should break his two carrier divisions out of Genda's box. But for the moment he could do nothing of the kind: He had to head all four carriers into the wind to receive planes as they returned from pounding Midway. The first of these appeared on the horizon as the last Vindicator dive bomber took a swipe at the *Akagi.* The recovery would consume some 40 precious minutes. More than another hour would pass before the next strike—including the twice-rearmed torpedo planes—could be readied and launched against the American fleet. Nagumo was running out of time. Even as he appraised his situation, the *Yorktown* was launching a strike. Torpedo planes and dive bombers from the *Hornet* and the *Enterprise* were already on the way.

Torpedo Squadron 8 from the *Hornet* reached the enemy first, but not without difficulty. Nagumo's carriers, having turned northeastward to recover their planes and get ready for their next attack, were not where they were expected to be. When Torpedo 8 found an expanse of empty sea instead of ships, Jack Waldron decided to search to the north. At about 9:25 a.m., he spied smoke above the horizon; it came from the stacks of Nagumo's ships.

Torpedo 8 had become separated from its fighter escort during the 2-hour-and-20-minute flight from the *Hornet.* To gain a tactical advantage over enemy Zeros, the American fighters flew thousands of feet higher than the Devastators. Separated by clouds, the two groups had drifted apart. Waldron knew that if he was to attack he would have to do it without his escort. Surely his men could get a hit or two in an audacious attack. He rocked his wings, signaling the squadron to close up for protection as they headed for the carrier *Kaga.*

Almost immediately, Zeros were upon them and the TBDs began dropping in flames. Waldron perished early. A shell ignited his fuel tank, and his plane blazed up. As he stood up to bail out, the aircraft slammed into the waves. Lumbering along at less than 200 miles per hour, every one of the 15 Devastators succumbed to the murderous 20-millimeter cannon fire of the far faster Zeros—or to bursts of antiaircraft fire from the ships. Abercrombie, Moore, Gay, all plummeted into the sea. Miraculously, however, Gay managed to climb out of his smoking

Midway in miniature

Photographers covering the Pacific war faced what was in every sense a large-scale problem. Because carrier battles spanned vast distances, even airborne cameras failed to capture the panoramic sweep of the action. *Life's* editors hit upon an innovative solution: They simply made the war small enough to photograph, commissioning an industrial designer to create room-sized scale models with plaster seascapes, cotton clouds, and miniature ships and planes.

Among the convincingly realistic results were photographs of models that depicted the Battle of Midway, reproduced here and on the following pages. They provide what on-the-scene photographers could not—comprehensive aerial views of carrier forces in action.

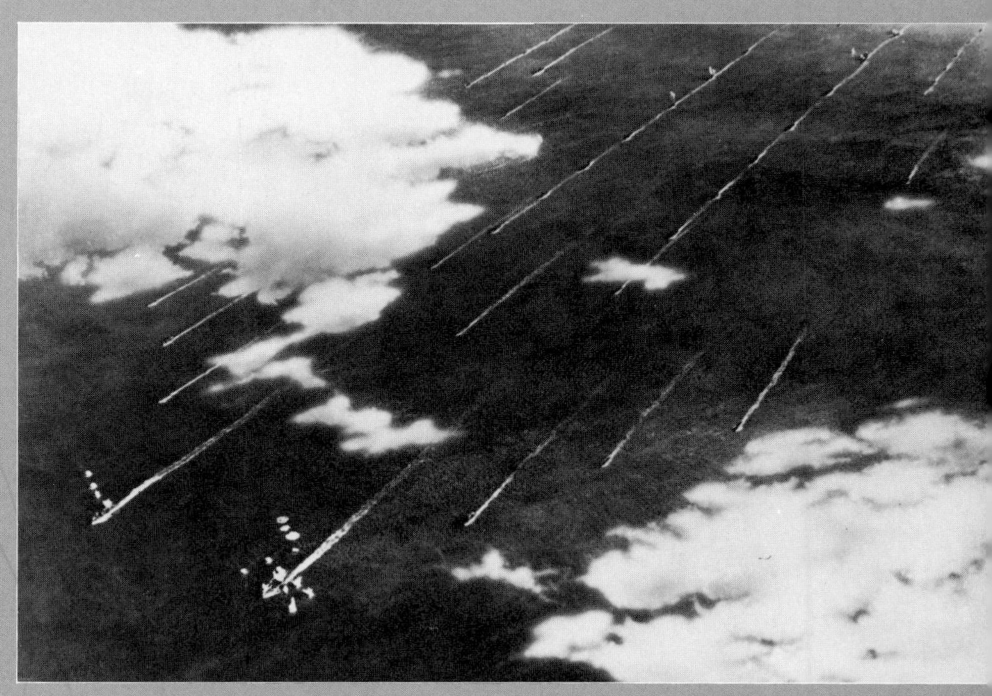

Unfazed by American bombs, the Japanese invasion fleet heads toward Midway.

wreckage before it sank. Though wounded, he grabbed hold of a floating seat cushion and held on to it, bobbing in the water as the enemy ships maneuvered all around him.

Lindsey and the 14 TBDs from the *Enterprise* arrived just in time to see Torpedo 8 obliterated. Though he, too, had lost his fighters, he ordered Torpedo 6 to attack at about 9:40. The Devastators bored in toward the *Kaga.* Zeros jumped on them, and few of the TBDs succeeded in launching their torpedoes. The torpedoes that were launched passed harmlessly by the *Kaga's* stern as she turned to avoid them.

Zeros and a furious barrage of flak from the *Kaga's* defensive screen of ships shot down Lindsey and nine of his fellows; two crewmen swam clear and were later rescued. The four remaining Devastators managed to escape and head home.

Nagumo was not able to launch his own strike while the enemy attacks were still going on, but his crews continued to refuel and rearm their planes. A third attack began at 10 a.m., when the *Yorktown's* Torpedo 3, under Lieutenant Commander Lance Massey, arrived on the scene. From high above, Thach's six Wildcats had kept the *Yorktown's* 12 TBDs in sight and were in a position to protect them as they approached the Japanese ships. But then a horde of Zeros set upon the American fighters, and Thach's men were soon weaving frantically for their own lives. Deprived of his escort, Massey followed the same instincts that had guided Waldron and Lindsey. He went for the *Soryu* as half a dozen Zeros swept in. Massey's plane caught fire and

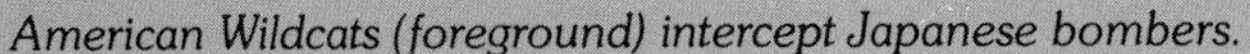

American Wildcats (foreground) intercept Japanese bombers.

Streaking in from above, planes attack the airfield on Midway.

went down. Most of the other Devastators soon followed him into the sea. Only two planes managed to escape. The *Soryu* was unscathed.

The Americans had now sent 93 bombers and torpedo planes against the Japanese. Not one had scored a hit.

In the lull that followed, Admiral Nagumo cocked his counterattack for launch, and at 10:24 the first Zero rolled down the deck of the *Akagi* and into the air. Commander Mitsuo Fuchida, still recovering from his appendectomy, was lying propped up at the flight command post and was relieved to see the flight finally get under way. But "at that instant," he remembered, "a lookout screamed: 'Dive bombers!' " While the Zeros had been disposing of the TBDs at masthead level and tangling with Thach's F4Fs, Max Leslie's two squadrons of Dauntlesses from the *Yorktown* and Wade McClusky's two from the *Enterprise* had come upon the radarless Japanese fleet unnoticed. "I've found the Jap," McClusky radioed his ship.

Assigning a different target to each of his two squadrons, McClusky led Scouting 6 against the *Kaga,* diving on the carrier unopposed. His pilots could scarcely believe their good fortune. At 10:22, his bomb struck the water 10 yards from the *Kaga.* The next two were also near misses, but then four bombs struck the ship in quick succession. One exploded amid the planes preparing to take off, and another penetrated to the hangar deck. Planes and ordnance detonated in a series of violent shocks. A small gasoline truck exploded, killing the captain and others on the bridge.

Circling wildly, the carrier Soryu is attacked by American dive bombers from Midway as her Zeros (foreground) try in vain to defend her.

Most of the Dauntlesses of Bombing 6 had mistakenly joined Scouting 6's attack on the *Kaga*. But the rest roared down on the *Akagi*. Commander Fuchida, at the lookout's warning, "looked up to see three black enemy planes plummeting toward our ship. The plump silhouettes of the American Dauntless dive bombers quickly grew larger, and then a number of black objects suddenly floated eerily from their wings. Bombs! Down they came straight toward me!" Fuchida instinctively took cover and escaped injury from the two bombs that smashed the *Akagi*. One hit the side of an elevator well; the other tore into the flight deck, repeating the devastation wreaked on the *Kaga*.

As McClusky's 30 SBDs strained for altitude after their attacks on the two ships, the Zeros and antiaircraft fire caught them. American rear-seat gunners managed to shoot down or drive off some of the Japanese planes, but no fewer than 14 Dauntlesses tumbled into the sea or ditched amid the enemy fleet. One of the downed crews managed to ditch safely and stay afloat in their inflated raft: Ensign Frank W. O'Flaherty and Bruno Gaido, the intrepid gunner who had engaged a Japanese bomber from a parked SBD about four months earlier.

Simultaneously with the attacks by the *Enterprise* squadrons, Max Leslie at the head of a *Yorktown* flight of 17 Dauntlesses peeled off at 14,500 feet over the *Soryu*. He no longer had a bomb; it had been prematurely released by a faulty arming mechanism shortly after takeoff, as had the bombs in three other SBDs. The four aircraft strafed the carrier to suppress flak for the planes that still

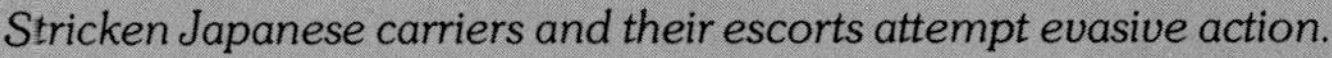

Stricken Japanese carriers and their escorts attempt evasive action.

As the Japanese retreat, diving Dauntlesses claim the cruiser Mogami.

had bombs. Leslie's wingman, Lieutenant Paul Holmberg, released his 1,000-pound bomb at the big, red Rising Sun painted on the *Soryu's* flight deck. The missile scored a bull's-eye. Of the other bombs aimed at the *Soryu,* 10 missed the carrier, but two more smashed into the flight deck, detonating fully loaded planes and carelessly stowed bombs. The Zeros were still preoccupied with McClusky's squadrons, and the surprised Japanese gunners on the *Soryu* failed to down even one SBD of Leslie's Bombing 3. The vessel appeared a total loss, so the pilots of the last four bombers aimed at large escort ships instead but apparently scored no hits.

High above the blazing ships, Thach's six Wildcat pilots had found themselves "inside a beehive" of Zeros, as Thach recalled. One F4F fell in flames, and as Thach turned to fire at an enemy plane, his wingman, Ensign Robert Dibb, called on the radio, "Skipper, there's a Zero on my tail. Get him off!"

Dibb knew his Thach weave. He "used his bean and swung in the right direction," said Thach, "leading the Zero around so I could shoot him." Thach "waited until he got fairly close, and we both opened up together, almost colliding. In the nick of time he lifted his left wing and just slid over one side of my fuselage. I got a glance at the belly of his plane, and it was smoking, with red flames coming out. He'd missed me."

Thach coached his team by radio through a series of such encounters. At least six Zeros were downed, and only one Wildcat was lost;

the weaving maneuver had worked splendidly. The remaining Zero pilots broke off the fight, seemingly stunned at the sight of their burning flattops below.

The American attack, concluded by 10:30, had left three Japanese carriers ablaze. Admiral Nagumo refused to shift the flag from the helpless *Akagi* until he was removed almost forcibly and taken to the cruiser *Nagara.* Commander Fuchida, who broke both ankles jumping to safety, was also taken to the *Nagara.* So was Commander Genda. Of Nagumo's four carriers, only the *Hiryu,* some miles to the north, had not been attacked.

The American carriers, meanwhile, were retrieving the planes and pilots that had survived the raid. Thach's group landed back on the *Yorktown* just after 10 SBDs of Scouting 5 had been launched to look for the *Hiryu.* At about noon, as Max Leslie's Bombing 3 approached to land, the planes were abruptly waved away. "Stand by to repel enemy air attack!" blared the ship's loudspeaker. "All hands lie down on deck. Air department take cover. Gunnery department take over." Radar had picked up a flight of bogeys 46 miles out and closing. It was a strike of 18 Val dive bombers and six Zeros from the *Hiryu,* launched an hour earlier by the aggressive Rear Admiral Tamon Yamaguchi, to whom Nagumo had passed command of air operations. Lieutenant Michio Kobayashi, the flight leader, had spotted Leslie's bombers and followed them back to their ship.

A dozen Wildcats patrolling over the *Yorktown* sped toward the intruders. Captain Elliott Buckmaster began to swing the ship, and the antiaircraft guns opened up at the approaching planes.

Yorktown's Wildcats tore into the bomb-laden Vals. Lieutenant William Barnes went for the lead Val at 12,000 feet: "I came in on him on a high side run. My guns were wide open and ripping into him. He went down smoking." Barnes used the same tactic on a second Japanese bomber, "boring down on him from the side and shooting him to pieces." After he had bagged a third, "three Zeros got on my tail and it was nip and tuck as I worked down to 9,000 feet and then dove off through a big cloud layer for about 2,000 feet to shake them off." He made it to the *Hornet,* his Wildcat full of holes.

The fighters and antiaircraft fire claimed 13 Vals and three Zeros at a cost of one Wildcat, but six of the enemy planes got through to release their 550-pound bombs. Buckmaster's skillful handling of the *Yorktown* enabled the ship to avoid three bombs, which just missed the stern, but not three others. One blew up on the flight deck, igniting fires that soon spread to lower decks. Two others penetrated the flight deck and exploded far below, one of them rupturing boiler flues and blowing out five of the ship's six boiler fires as if they were candles. The firerooms were quickly filled with choking stack gases. The *Yorktown* abruptly lost speed, from 30 knots to six knots, and then stopped altogether. At 1:15 p.m., Admiral Fletcher shifted his flag to the cruiser *Astoria.* But fire fighters soon got the flames under control, and by about 2 p.m. the *Yorktown's* damage-control parties had her speed up to 17 knots, with fighters on the deck being refueled for launch.

Before the Wildcats could be fully fueled, radar picked up more bogeys, and soon 10 torpedo-bearing Kates with an escort of six Zeros were sighted, heading for the *Yorktown.* They had been launched from the *Hiryu* as soon as the planes could be readied after the first strike had departed. The Kates attacked from four directions at once, in the face of fire from a dozen Wildcats on combat air patrol as well as antiaircraft fire from the *Yorktown* and her screen of cruisers and destroyers. Although about half the attackers plunged seaward in flames, five Kates got through. The carrier dodged some of their torpedoes, but two struck the port side. The explosions knocked out electrical power throughout the ship, engulfing all belowdecks compartments in inky darkness. The engines died, sea water poured in and the *Yorktown* developed a list to port that rapidly increased to 26 degrees. Fearing the ship would capsize, the captain ordered her abandoned.

The Americans were not to remain on the defensive for long. A few minutes earlier, at 2:45 p.m., a *Yorktown* scout dispatched before the first Japanese attack had reported sighting the *Hiryu.* Within an hour, Admiral Spruance launched two dozen SBDs from the *Enterprise,* including 14 of the *Yorktown's* planes that Max Leslie had brought aboard after being diverted from his own ship. The bombers arrived over the *Hiryu* at 5:00 p.m., again at the perfect moment. Yamaguchi, who had learned from a reconnaissance pilot that three American carriers were on hand for the battle, had assembled fully loaded planes on his flight deck for a twilight attack. Americans dived out of the sun and planted four 1,000-pound bombs squarely on the deck of the gyrating *Hiryu.* Two SBDs were lost to the half-dozen defending Zeros, but parked planes on the *Hiryu* erupted in steel-twisting explosions. Now all four Japanese carriers were ablaze.

Several hundred miles to the northwest, aboard the *Yamato,* Admiral Yamamoto heard the news with profound dismay. His carriers were finished. The *Soryu* would sink with 718 men at 7:15 that night. The *Kaga* would follow 10 minutes later with about 800 men. The *Akagi* would burn through the night, her dead numbering 221; she would be scuttled before dawn. The *Hiryu* would slip beneath the waves at 8:20 a.m., after a *coup de grâce* by Japanese destroyers. Admiral Yamaguchi, who insisted on staying on board, went down with her.

Yamamoto briefly considered calling in other forces, including the two light carriers, *Ryujo* and *Junyo,* that were taking part in the diversionary attack on the Aleutians, to make a final effort against Admiral Spruance and Task Force 16. But then he thought better of the idea, and at 2:55 a.m. on June 5 he issued an order: "The Midway operation is canceled." Except for follow-up American air strikes against Japanese ships as they withdrew westward—strikes that damaged the cruiser *Mogami* and sank the cruiser *Mikuma*—the Battle of Midway was over. Yamamoto had failed, his plan disrupted by the U.S. Navy's superior

Fire fighters hose down the Yorktown's decks after a Japanese dive-bomber attack at Midway on June 4, 1942. Although the carrier suffered three bomb hits, her captain and crew were on the verge of bringing the flames under control when the Japanese struck again.

Maneuvering under her protective barrage of antiaircraft fire, the Yorktown is struck amidships by a torpedo during the second Japanese air attack at Midway. Moments later, another torpedo slammed into her side, causing massive flooding and a complete loss of power.

intelligence, tactics—and luck. Four Japanese flattops and one heavy cruiser had been lost, along with some 2,500 men and 234 aircraft. All Yamamato had to show for his efforts was the occupation of Attu and Kiska Islands in the Aleutians, which would prove to be no more than a minor irritant to the Americans.

On June 5, a PBY Catalina plucked Ensign Gay, sole survivor of Torpedo 8, out of the Pacific. Hiding behind his seat cushion, he had avoided capture and witnessed the sinking of three of the Japanese carriers. Frank O'Flaherty of Scouting 6 and his gunner Bruno Gaido had also witnessed the events, but under even less pleasant circumstances—as prisoners aboard the destroyer *Makigumo.* According to testimony by Japanese officers after the War, they were interrogated for a week. Afterward, they were blindfolded, bound hand and foot, weighted with water-filled cans and flung overboard by their captors. In all 307 Americans were lost. In addition, 147 U.S. aircraft were destroyed during the battle, and one carrier and a destroyer sunk.

The tally of lost American ships very nearly did not include an aircraft carrier. The doughty *Yorktown* was reluctant to die. Her list soon stabilized at 25 degrees, the fires burned themselves out and the Americans began to think that perhaps the ship could be saved. On the afternoon of June 5 she was taken in tow by a minesweeper, and early the following morning the destroyer *Hammann* put Captain Buckmaster and a salvage party aboard.

By midafternoon, water pumped into the port side of *Yorktown's* hull had leveled the ship. But then the Japanese submarine *I-168* came upon the *Yorktown* and the *Hammann.* It slammed one torpedo into the destroyer, which broke in half and plunged straight to the bottom with a third of her 241-man crew. Two other torpedoes opened gaping holes in the *Yorktown.* She was mortally wounded. Some of the ship's internal telephones still worked, and a call went down to three enlisted men who were trapped far below. "Do you know what a fix you're in?" they were asked. "Sure," came the reply, "but what a hell of an acey-deucy game we're having down here right now." Her deck tilted more steeply toward the water, and the salvage party was taken off. On the morning of the 7th, the *Yorktown* rolled over and sank.

When the sea claimed the *Yorktown,* it swallowed up the last wreckage of the Battle of Midway. The losers set course for safety. "We are retreating," wrote one Japanese officer. "It is utterly discouraging."

The winners now prepared to exploit their victory. On June 6 the *Saratoga* arrived at Pearl Harbor from San Diego, the torpedo damage that had laid her up for five months fully repaired. The next day she put to sea to fly much-needed replacement pilots and planes to the *Enterprise* and *Hornet.* And on the 10th the carrier *Wasp,* which had been busy ferrying aircraft from Great Britain to Malta, passed through the Panama Canal into the Pacific. With four carriers to pit against Japan's *Zuikaku, Shokaku* and a handful of light carriers, the U.S. Pacific Fleet was equipped to take the offensive.

The trying choreography of the flight deck

An aircraft carrier's deck crews almost never made wartime headlines. Yet these hard-working "airedales" or "sheepdogs"—so called because they were constantly shepherding planes about the ship—performed risky and backbreaking jobs that were crucial to carrier victories.

To prepare for a launch, airedales from the carrier's Traffic Unit, also known as plane pushers or spotters, brought aircraft up from the hangar deck by elevator. With the help of small tractors, they then maneuvered each plane to its appropriate spot, or parking place, on the flight deck and secured it with chocks. Close on their heels, airedales from the ship's Gassing Unit fueled the planes, and ordnancemen armed them. During these operations, high winds sometimes threatened to sweep both men and machines overboard, deck hands were sitting ducks for attacks by enemy bombers and every aircraft was a potential tinderbox.

Once the pilots had manned their planes and started the engines, airedales faced an additional hazard: Moving about the crowded deck to release chocks, each crewman had to exercise the utmost caution to avoid being driven backward by the slip stream of one airplane into the spinning propeller of another. Meanwhile, airedales stationed at intervals along the deck used hand signals to coach taxiing planes forward to the launching officer. That official, carefully gauging the pitch and roll of the ship, selected the most favorable moment for each aircraft's takeoff.

When all the planes were in the air, the airedales could relax. Men often were so exhausted after the strenuous launching operation that they fell asleep on the deck. Others turned to books, wrote letters or whiled away the hours with games. Eventually, the distant drone of returning squadrons stirred the men to action once more, and a landing signal officer readied his brightly colored paddles to direct the approach of each incoming pilot.

Landings were by far the most dangerous part of flight-deck operations. When a plane crash-landed and burst into flames, airedales rushed in from the side lines to fight the fire with carbon dioxide, and asbestos-suited rescue teams freed fliers from the burning wreckage. Such courage earned the heartfelt admiration of carrier pilots and admirals alike. In the words of one naval officer, "a flight deck would not be, could not be, worth taking to sea without them."

Crews of airedales guide tractor-towed Hellcat fighters (lower right and center) toward a carrier's stern before a launch. Dauntless dive bombers are already spotted along the flight deck's edge (upper right).

Members of a gassing crew fuel a combat-bound Hellcat. Aviation fuel was pumped to the flight deck from huge tanks that, for ballasting purposes, were arranged along the ship's bottom.

Squatting on a Hellcat's wing, an ordnanceman loads a box of ammunition for one of the fighter's six .50-caliber machine guns while his assistant fills the next box with a belt of cartridges.

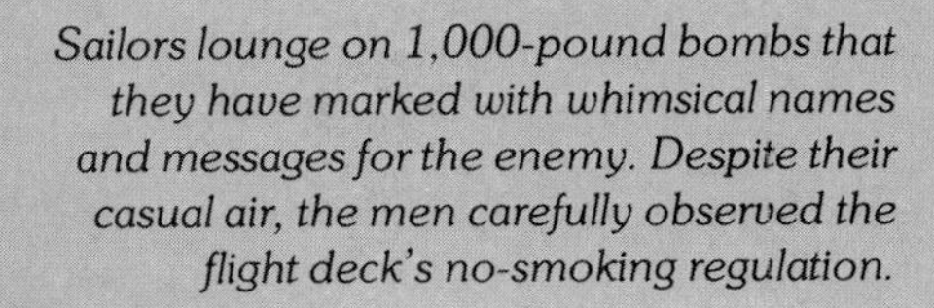

Sailors lounge on 1,000-pound bombs that they have marked with whimsical names and messages for the enemy. Despite their casual air, the men carefully observed the flight deck's no-smoking regulation.

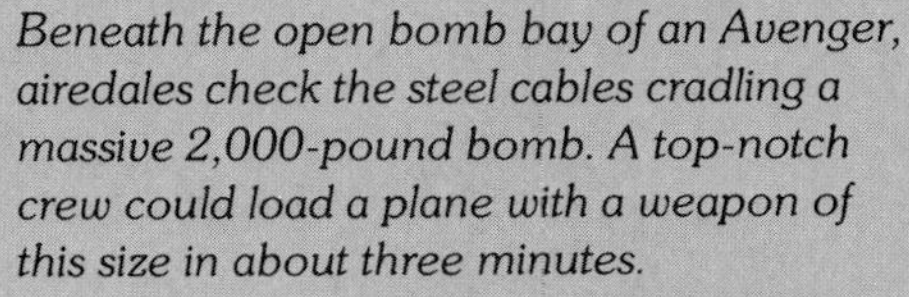

Beneath the open bomb bay of an Avenger, airedales check the steel cables cradling a massive 2,000-pound bomb. A top-notch crew could load a plane with a weapon of this size in about three minutes.

While an Avenger pilot starts his engine, an armament expert activates the firing mechanisms of four 5-inch rockets under the plane's starboard wing. To minimize the danger of accidental firing, this task was left until just before takeoff.

Preparing for departure, a pilot climbs into the cockpit of a Dauntless dive bomber ahead of his gunner. The airedales in the background are on hand to help them fasten their parachute harnesses.

While pilots rev their engines, deck hands steady the wings and stand by to pull out the chocks. During launch operations, crewmen kept the planes moving forward, one at a time, in a quick but regular rhythm.

As he leads a carrier plane through traffic on the flight deck, an airedale signals the pilot to taxi forward (below, left) and then raises his arms in the gesture that means "Hold it."

Communicating with a flag, a launching officer directs a dive-bomber pilot to "hold the brakes" until given the signal for takeoff. Because low-flying planes could be swamped by high seas, the moment of lift-off was timed to coincide with a rising deck.

In a blur of accelerating speed, a Hellcat roars off the flight deck as officers looking on from the carrier's island shield their ears against the noise. Under optimum conditions, the next plane would be launched within 20 or 30 seconds.

After a launch, exhausted airedales nap on the flight deck. The crane attached to the rubber-tired tractor was used to rapidly clear the deck of wrecked planes.

Deck crews pass the time with mumblety-peg, a game in which the players flipped a knife from various positions in an attempt to lodge its blade in the wooden deck.

Their rest over, airedales bring out the chocks for returning planes. In rough weather stout ropes were used to secure aircraft to the flight deck.

Having signaled a pilot to cut his throttle, a landing signal officer watches carefully as the aircraft lands. Part of the LSO's job was to evaluate each pilot's technique and teach correct landing habits.

Airedales disengage a Wildcat's tail hook from one of the flight deck's arresting wires. To reduce the chance of accidents, the pilot was not permitted to leave his plane until its wheels had been chocked into place.

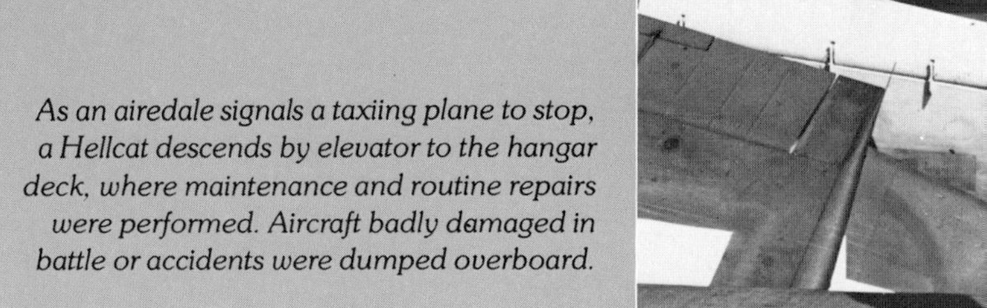

As an airedale signals a taxiing plane to stop, a Hellcat descends by elevator to the hangar deck, where maintenance and routine repairs were performed. Aircraft badly damaged in battle or accidents were dumped overboard.

Clothed in asbestos from head to foot, fire fighters watch landing operations intently, ready to spring into action if a plane should crash and burst into flames.

Shouting orders, a deck officer exhorts his team of airedales to wrestle a damaged plane out of the way in a hurry so that other returning aircraft can land.

Two fire fighters clamber up onto the wing of a burning Helldiver to rescue the fliers as others move in to extinguish the blaze with carbon dioxide.

4

Collisions on the road to Tokyo

Six weeks after the Americans turned the tables on the Japanese at Midway, the carriers *Saratoga, Wasp* and *Enterprise,* under the command of Admiral Fletcher, were slicing northward through the Coral Sea in company with most of Admiral Nimitz' Pacific Fleet. "The horizon was littered with ships," remembered Avenger pilot Fred Mears, reassigned from the *Hornet* to the *Enterprise* after Midway. "All over the sea, and as far out as eye could reach, the armada mottled the water."

The *Enterprise* and her sister flattops were part of a plan to recover the Solomon Islands and then evict the Japanese from their major base at Rabaul, on New Britain in the Bismarck Archipelago. The carriers would provide air support for landings by a division of Marines, whose first objectives were Guadalcanal and Tulagi. The Japanese had seized Tulagi days before the Battle of the Coral Sea and later had started building an airfield on neighboring Guadalcanal—a project the Americans were determined not to let them complete. At present, Rabaul was the Japanese fighter and bomber base nearest to vulnerable Allied supply lines leading through the New Hebrides to Australia. An airfield at Guadalcanal would be 650 miles closer—and that much deadlier.

After supper on August 6, the eve of the assault, the air officer aboard the *Enterprise* wound up his briefing with some grimly worded advice: "Show no quarter," he told Mears and the rest of Air Group 6. "Don't hesitate to be absolutely ruthless. You can be sure you will receive the same treatment." Then he added, "For eight months now we have been on the defensive. Tomorrow the tide is going to turn."

And so it would, but slowly and at a terrible cost. In the summer of 1942, Japan still had a formidable fleet. As the U.S. forces began their advance, Japan implemented its long-standing defensive strategy—to exhaust the enemy's armies while diminishing its fleet to a size that Japan's warships could defeat in a decisive battle. That battle would come two years later. For the moment, Guadalcanal would demonstrate Japan's ability and determination to wage a war of attrition.

U.S. cruisers and destroyers began to bombard Japanese fortifications on the island shortly after 6 a.m. on August 7. At about the same

Silhouetted against the clouds, a U.S. Navy Dauntless dive bomber prepares to attack Japanese positions on Wake Island at the start of America's offensive in the Central Pacific in 1943.

time, the first fighters and dive bombers took off from the carriers to strike the airstrip a-building at Lunga Point, on Guadalcanal's northern coast. The attack took the Japanese completely by surprise: Marines swarming ashore met virtually no opposition. By the next afternoon, the airstrip—soon renamed Henderson Field—was in American hands, although Japanese ground forces still occupied most of the island. Stronger resistance, however, was encountered on Tulagi, where the Japanese held out for more than 30 hours.

The skies were relatively peaceful at first. Fighter pilot Joseph Daly later wrote that the morning flight off the *Saratoga* returned with "nothing to report except the slaughter of 10 cows which one of the boys had mowed down with his machine gun"; he had mistaken them for a troop of Japanese infantry. But bigger game would soon appear.

Shortly after noon, Daly's squadron of Wildcats was in the air over the channel between Tulagi and Guadalcanal, flying combat air patrol for the transports disgorging the Marines. At 1:20, enemy planes were spotted approaching at 12,000 feet. The Americans had been expecting Japanese bombers from Rabaul, and now they had arrived: 27 twin-engined Bettys, flying in a solid V-formation. Daly and another pilot, William "Wild Bill" Holt, pushed over and attacked.

"As I closed in on them with all machine-guns blazing," Daly wrote, "a thin line of gray smoke tailed each plane—their turret gunners were all firing back at me." Daly's twisting Wildcat was hit, but not seriously, and he managed to knock down two of the bombers in four attempts; Holt scored once. As Daly positioned his Wildcat for a fifth pass at the bombers, he noticed two planes far to the rear and coming up fast. Thinking they were friendly, he continued lining up on the bombers. Then he realized the planes were Zero fighters that had traveled the 650 miles from Rabaul. "It didn't seem possible that a fighter could fly such a distance and return," Daly wrote. "We live and learn." As he turned to face his pursuers, his Wildcat was hit by a 20-millimeter shell, and flames engulfed the cockpit. Though badly burned, Daly managed to bail out; he was rescued a couple of hours later by a seaplane on antisubmarine patrol.

The Japanese fliers from Rabaul had not grappled with American carrier pilots before, and—despite their advantage of surprise— this first encounter came as a rude shock. The evasive Thach weave confused them, and the aggressiveness of the American airmen gave them pause. One clash caused Flight Petty Officer Saburo Sakai, a leading Japanese ace, to gape in wonder. "A single Wildcat pursued three Zero fighters," he wrote afterward, "firing in short bursts at the frantic Japanese planes. All four planes were in a wild dogfight, flying tight left spirals. The Zeros should have been able to take the lone Grumman without any trouble, but every time a Zero caught the Wildcat before its guns, the enemy plane flipped away wildly and came out again on the tail of a Zero. I had never seen such flying before."

Sakai himself went after this bold American pilot and after a fierce

A nemesis of American carrier pilots, Saburo Sakai scored a grand total of 64 aerial kills—a record that he attributed in part to his Samurai ancestry. He was one of the handful of Japanese aces to survive the War.

dogfight shot him down. Next, Sakai set an SBD Dauntless ablaze, then turned to pursue a flight of what he took for eight Wildcats. Since a Wildcat mounted no guns that fired to the rear, he came up beneath them for a safe shot from astern—only to have .30- and .50-caliber slugs rip into his Zero. Sakai had jumped a formation of TBF Avengers, new torpedo planes with turret-mounted and stinger machine guns, the latter named for their location near the tail of the plane. Sakai broke off his attack, but not before he was badly wounded in the head. Despite his injuries, he managed to keep his crippled fighter in the air until he could reach Rabaul. Though permanently blinded in one eye, he would eventually return to active duty and would fight on until the War's end.

Three days of air attacks from Rabaul cost the Japanese 42 planes—and, more seriously, 42 veteran pilots. Some were shot down; most, having overreached their range in flying from Rabaul, were simply swallowed up by the sea. Of the bombers that participated, less than half returned and for all their efforts, the U.S. build-up on Guadalcanal barely slowed. American aircraft losses totaled 11 Wildcats (six of them shot down by Japan's top ace, Warrant Officer Hiroyoshi Nishizawa) and the Dauntless destroyed by Sakai.

It was Japanese sea power that very nearly thwarted the Americans on Guadalcanal. In the early hours of August 9, Vice Admiral Gunichi Mikawa led a force of seven cruisers and one destroyer toward the island. His purpose was to destroy the screen of warships—including two Australian cruisers—protecting the American transports anchored offshore, then to sink the transports, too.

The destroyer *Patterson* detected Mikawa's squadron near Savo Island, about eight miles north of Guadalcanal, at 1:43 a.m. Seconds later Japanese cannon opened fire. Benefiting from a variety of factors—the element of surprise, an unfortunate disposition of American ships because of the need to guard four approaches to Guadalcanal, failure of communications among the Allied squadron and Japanese superiority in fighting sea battles at night—Mikawa dealt the enemy a humiliating defeat. Four cruisers were sunk and 1,023 men lost their lives. By 2:30 a.m., little more than a rain squall or two stood between Mikawa and his enemy's supply ships. But instead of attacking, he pulled back, fearing retaliation from Fletcher's flattops at daybreak.

In fact, Fletcher was out of the picture, having withdrawn his carriers southeastward the preceding evening. Even before the assault on Guadalcanal, Fletcher had announced that he would keep his carriers on station for no more than two days at a time, and none of his superiors had contradicted him. Still smarting from the loss of the *Lexington* and the *Yorktown* earlier that year, Fletcher believed that longer stays would leave his flattops too vulnerable to Japanese air attack. Because of his caution, his Avengers and Dauntlesses were too far from the action to attack Mikawa's ships as they retreated. Consequently, the Japanese got away virtually unscathed.

Fifteen days later the Imperial Navy took on the Allies again. This time

Admiral Yamamoto ordered more than 60 ships to Guadalcanal, where they were to batter whatever enemy warships they could engage and land a contingent of 1,500 troops to bolster the island's garrison. To protect the battleships and cruisers from ambush by Fletcher's carriers, Yamamoto committed his own flattops to battle for the first time since Midway. His plan was to bait a trap for the American carriers with the light carrier *Ryujo.* When they struck, planes from the fast carriers *Zuikaku* and *Shokaku* would counterattack and sink them.

On the morning of August 24, American reconnaissance planes spotted the *Ryujo* 280 miles northwest of Fletcher's two carriers, the *Enterprise* and the *Saratoga.* (The previous evening Fletcher, not expecting a battle so soon, had sent the *Wasp* and her supporting ships to be refueled.) Fletcher steamed toward the *Ryujo* and launched 61 Dauntlesses and Avengers against Yamamoto's bait. Commander Harry D. Felt led the *Saratoga's* contingent, 38 aircraft strong. He hit the target with a 1,000-pound bomb, one of at least four—and perhaps as many as 10—that struck home. No sooner had the dive bombers finished their work than five Avengers attacked the Japanese carrier on both sides of the bow. Only one of their torpedoes found its mark but, combined with the bomb damage, it was enough to sink the *Ryujo.* Remarkably, not a single American plane was lost in the action.

Just 15 minutes after Admiral Fletcher launched his attacks against the *Ryujo,* he learned of the presence of the *Shokaku* and the *Zuikaku,* but there was little he could do about them. Already, they were preparing to launch air strikes against him. Most of his bombers and torpedo planes had already been committed against the *Ryujo,* and attempts to divert them to the new targets failed because of poor radio reception that day.

At two minutes past four p.m., a horde of bogeys appeared on American radar screens. Wildcats, armed and warmed up in anticipation of the attack, scrambled to join other fighters already flying combat air patrol. In all, 53 Wildcats formed the reception committee, but only a few of them managed to penetrate a defensive screen of Zeros to attack the Val dive bombers approaching the *Enterprise* and the *Saratoga.* Ensign Donald Runyon, a Wildcat section leader aboard the *Enterprise,* was one who succeeded. Tearing out of the sun, Runyon opened fire on a Val that had not seen him. The Japanese plane exploded in mid-air. Repeating the tactic, Runyon blew up another Val, then a Zero that attempted to intervene, and then a third Val.

While Runyon chipped away at the periphery of the Japanese attack, the center pressed on toward the *Enterprise.* (The *Saratoga,* operating 10 miles away, would be ignored this day.) At 4:41 p.m., the first Val attacked, nosing into a screaming dive. Behind it, at seven-second intervals, followed two dozen more. The first bomb splashed into the water alongside the *Enterprise,* a dud. Aboard the carrier and her attendant ships, every gun that could be brought to bear peppered the sky with shells, and at least six Vals succumbed to the

Hydraulic assists for takeoff and landing

Though most carrier takeoffs were made with a rolling start, the use of catapults became commonplace as the War progressed. These hydraulic launching machines—schematically explained in the top two diagrams at right—gave a carrier commander important advantages in a fray. Because the catapults could launch planes from a deck loaded with battle-ready aircraft, they enabled the commander to dispatch his flight group very quickly. Moreover, they permitted him to send planes aloft without first turning the carrier into the wind, a procedure that could route the ship toward the enemy. Catapults also allowed him to launch planes at night without turning on any telltale lights.

In addition to machinery to put planes in the air, the carriers had hydraulically cushioned arresting cables to catch planes when they landed *(bottom diagrams).* If a plane missed the cables, it was jerked to a halt by emergency barriers. After each successful landing, the barriers were laid flat on the deck to allow the plane to taxi forward.

This portrait of the Yorktown is striped with red lines to show arresting-cable positions, blue lines to indicate emergency barriers and yellow lines to mark the carrier's twin catapults.

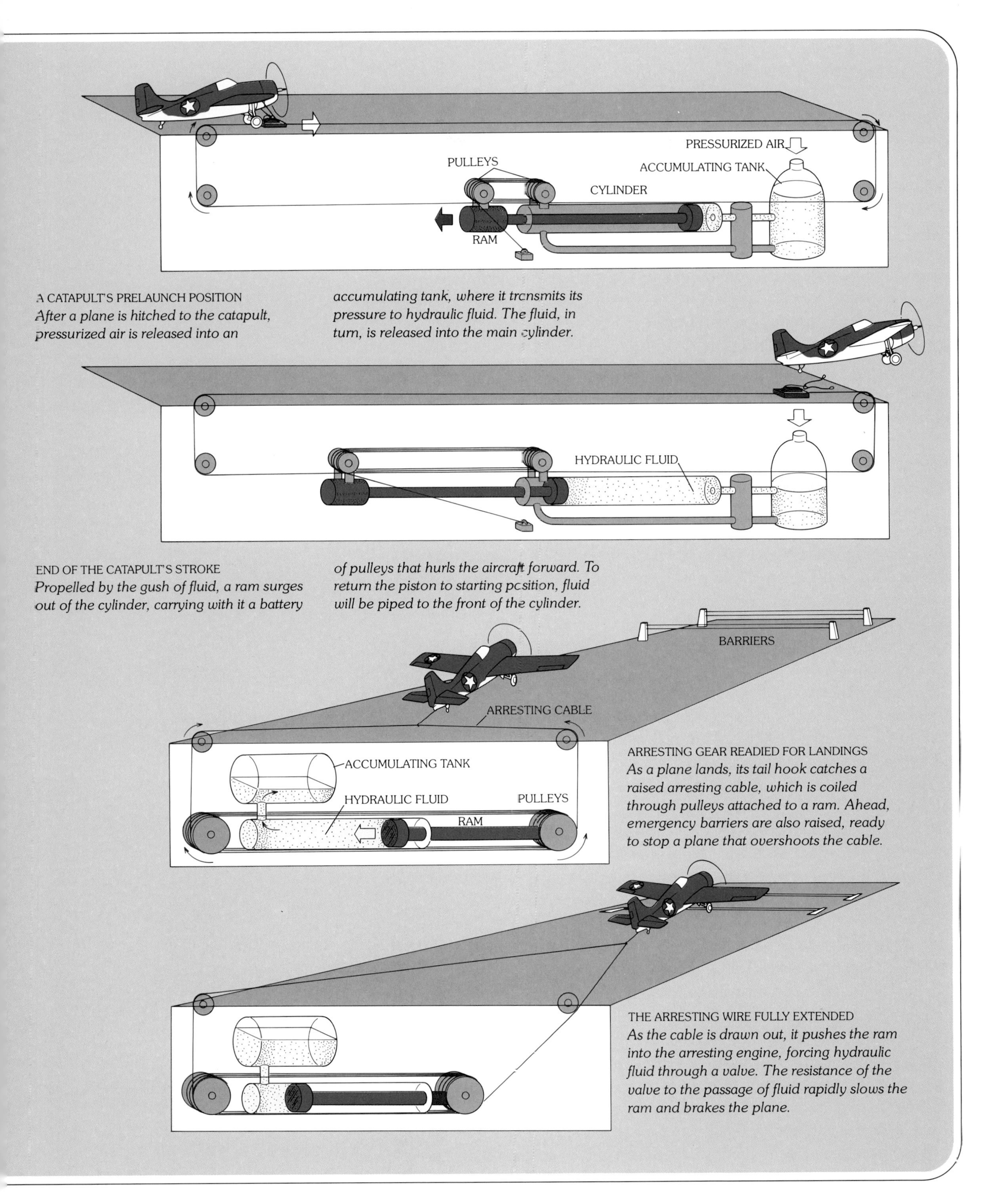

A CATAPULT'S PRELAUNCH POSITION
After a plane is hitched to the catapult, pressurized air is released into an accumulating tank, where it transmits its pressure to hydraulic fluid. The fluid, in turn, is released into the main cylinder.

END OF THE CATAPULT'S STROKE
Propelled by the gush of fluid, a ram surges out of the cylinder, carrying with it a battery of pulleys that hurls the aircraft forward. To return the piston to starting position, fluid will be piped to the front of the cylinder.

ARRESTING GEAR READIED FOR LANDINGS
As a plane lands, its tail hook catches a raised arresting cable, which is coiled through pulleys attached to a ram. Ahead, emergency barriers are also raised, ready to stop a plane that overshoots the cable.

THE ARRESTING WIRE FULLY EXTENDED
As the cable is drawn out, it pushes the ram into the arresting engine, forcing hydraulic fluid through a valve. The resistance of the valve to the passage of fluid rapidly slows the ram and brakes the plane.

devastating fire. But three of the dive bombers scored hits that ignited fires in the aft part of the ship.

From the air, the *Enterprise* appeared to be grievously wounded—licked by flames and emitting clouds of black smoke. However, the fires were quickly brought under control, and the flight deck, perforated by bombs that had detonated several decks below, was temporarily patched with metal plates. Within an hour of the last explosion, the *Enterprise* was steaming into the wind at 24 knots, ready to recover her aircraft.

In this, the Battle of the Eastern Solomons, Fletcher had stolen Yamamoto's bait. Because the Japanese fast carriers had failed to establish air superiority over Guadalcanal, they and the rest of the fleet retired without delivering their cargo of troops to the island.

The situation on the island had reached something of an impasse. Seabees had completed the airstrip at Henderson Field, but at night, when U.S. planes were powerless to intervene, the Japanese ferried supplies and troops by speedy destroyers to strengthen their hold on the rest of the island. So regular were these shipping runs that the Marines nicknamed them the Tokyo Express. More often than not, they were punctuated by Japanese naval gunfire and air raids that kept the Marines ducking all night. By dawn each day, the destroyers had pulled out, and the Americans proceeded to reinforce their own garrison. At the end of August, more than 16,000 American troops on Guadalcanal were facing some 8,000 Japanese, and neither force could defeat the other.

The *Enterprise,* though admirably patched up after the battle, was in no shape for combat and had to put in at Pearl Harbor for repairs. The *Saratoga* and the *Wasp*—soon joined by the *Hornet,* which had come from Pearl after training operations—patrolled southeast of Guadalcanal, beyond the range of Japanese reconnaissance aircraft based at Rabaul.

Though secure from air attack, the carriers were vulnerable to enemy submarines. On August 31, the *Saratoga's* radar showed a suspicious blip. The destroyer *Farragut* sped to the vicinity of the contact but failed to detect the threat that lurked below—Japanese submarine *I-26.* As the *Saratoga's* sailors lined up for breakfast, the *I-26* fired six torpedoes at the carrier. Alerted by a submarine-warning flag raised on another destroyer, Captain Dewitt Ramsey, the carrier's skipper, ordered engines to full speed and began a ponderous evasive turn. Five of the torpedoes passed by, but the sixth planted itself in the *Saratoga's* starboard side near the island. Fortunately, the explosion wounded only a dozen men and killed none. Moreover, structural damage to the *Saratoga* proved to be minor, and she steamed safely to Tongatabu, a Navy base near the Fiji Islands, to have her hull made sound again.

The Japanese submarines were not through. On September 15, as the *Wasp* completed launching combat-air-patrol and antisubmarine sorties, lookouts spotted torpedo wakes lancing toward the ship. Sub-

Oily smoke mushrooms up from the Wasp after it was torpedoed by a Japanese submarine on September 15, 1942, while supporting the American landings on Guadalcanal. The Wasp was the third U.S. carrier lost in action during the first year of the Pacific war.

marine *I-19* had foiled all six of the destroyers in the *Wasp's* escort and had loosed a pattern of four torpedoes. Three of them ripped into the hull. The explosions were tremendous, lifting aircraft off the deck and wrenching heavy generators from their mounts. Fires spread quickly through hoses still plump with aviation fuel and threatened aircraft loaded with bombs. Worst of all, the detonations ruptured water mains; at critical points, fire-fighting equipment was inoperable. Gradually, the fires gained the upper hand. The order was given to abandon ship; after the evacuation, the destroyer *Lansdowne* delivered the *coup de grâce* with torpedoes. At 9:00 the *Wasp* went under.

The attacks by submarines, plus the three bombs that had disabled the *Enterprise* in the Battle of the Eastern Solomons, reduced the number of serviceable American aircraft carriers in the Pacific to a single ship—the *Hornet*. And she was outnumbered 5 to 1. In addition to the fast carriers *Shokaku* and *Zuikaku*, the Japanese had three light carriers:

the *Zuiho,* a ship of prewar vintage, and the *Hiyo* and *Junyo,* both merchant-ship conversions completed in 1942. Of the three, only the *Junyo* had seen action; she had been part of the unsuccessful diversion that preceded the Battle of Midway.

Yamamoto intended to put his carrier advantage to good use in the continuing battle for Guadalcanal. Certainly the stakes were high enough: The island's airfield was still in the hands of the Americans, and unless they could be driven off, all of Japan's conquests in the southern Pacific would be in jeopardy.

The admiral and his counterparts in the Army worked out a bold plan. Japanese Army troops and Marines were to assault and capture Henderson Field on October 22. Simultaneously, the Imperial Navy's battleships and aircraft carriers were to prevent any American reinforcements from reaching the island. Once the airfield was in friendly hands, the operations order directed the ships "to apprehend and annihilate any powerful forces in the Solomons area."

The Japanese ground forces, however, failed to do their part. Though wave upon wave of troops crashed upon the defense perimeter around Henderson Field, the Americans held their ground, and by October 26 all the vigor had gone out of the Japanese attack. Japan's losses numbered in the thousands, whereas the defenders suffered only 156 dead and four missing in action.

The failure of the Japanese forces to quickly capture the airfield had far-reaching consequences. In American hands, Henderson Field posed a threat to Japanese aircraft carriers operating near the Solomons, and according to Yamamoto's plan, Admiral Nagumo, in charge of the flattops, ought to have withdrawn when the attempt to seize the airfield bogged down. But he loitered in the area and eventually was discovered by patrolling PBYs based on the island of Espiritu Santo.

Meanwhile, the Americans' capacity to deal with the Japanese had improved remarkably. On October 24, the *Enterprise* had rejoined the *Hornet.* This doubled the strength of the carrier force, now under Rear Admiral Thomas C. Kinkaid, with Vice Admiral William Halsey, commander of South Pacific Forces, overseeing operations from Nouméa. Moreover, though Kinkaid and Halsey were unaware of the fact, the *Hiyo* had been forced by balky engines to return to Truk. Thus, over the span of a few days, the odds against the U.S. carriers had improved from a staggering 5 to 1 to an almost rosy 2 to 1.

Snoopers from both forces were in the air early on October 26, but Kinkaid had the first luck. At 6:50 a.m., two *Enterprise* scout planes—Dauntlesses armed with 500-pound bombs in case they came upon the enemy—sighted Nagumo's carriers northwest of the Santa Cruz Islands and less than 200 miles from the American flattop. As the two planes climbed into position to start a bombing attack, eight Zeros appeared, chasing them away from the carriers and forcing them to hide in the clouds. Rear-seat gunners in the dive bombers knocked down three of their assailants, and the Dauntlesses escaped unscathed.

Stalking U-boats in the Atlantic

"I will show that the U-boat alone can win this war," promised German Admiral Karl Dönitz in 1940. He came close to proving his boast as his submarine wolf packs slashed at the Atlantic shipping that kept the Allies' European war effort alive. During a single month in 1943, U-boats sent some 620,000 tons of vital supplies to the ocean floor.

Dönitz' U-boats operated well out of range of counterattacks by land-based planes; only carrierborne aircraft could reach them. Because U.S. flattops were committed to operations against Japan in the Pacific, the Navy in 1942 began converting merchant vessels into small escort carriers for antisubmarine duty in the Atlantic. Each of these "baby flattops" carried up to 24 aircraft—Avenger torpedo planes and Wildcat fighters—and sailed in company with three to six sub-hunting destroyers.

The first of the new escort carriers was the U.S.S. *Bogue*, which entered service in February 1943. For two months the *Bogue* group steamed inside Atlantic convoys without encountering any submarines. Then, in a new offensive approach, the Navy designated the *Bogue* and her destroyers a hunter-killer group, and the Avengers and Wildcats were paired in wide-ranging search teams that stalked U-boats independently of the convoys. When the pilots caught a submarine on the surface, they blasted it with an assortment of weapons *(overleaf)*. If the quarry gained refuge beneath the waves, they called in the group's destroyers, which struck at the submarine with depth charges.

Within days of adopting this aggressive technique, the *Bogue* group sank one U-boat, damaged two and chased away another pair. By the spring of 1944, eleven such teams of carriers and destroyers had virtually eliminated enemy submarines from the shipping lanes of the Atlantic Ocean.

The U.S.S. Bogue, America's first small, sub-hunting escort carrier, cruises a calm Atlantic as a Wildcat fighter circles overhead.

On the Bogue's flight deck, the crew of an Avenger prepares for takeoff in May 1944. This versatile warplane assaulted U-boats with rockets (under the wing), machine guns and depth charges that were set to hit U-boats on or near the surface.

Four Wildcat fighters from the Bogue scout the Atlantic for enemy submarines. In an attack, Wildcats strafed subs to chase antiaircraft gunners from their posts and provide a safe approach for the more heavily armed Avengers.

In June 1943, German sailors scramble for cover during an attack on their submarine, the U-118, by aircraft from the Bogue.

To confirm their kill, low-flying Avenger torpedo planes from the Bogue circle the spot where the U-118 went down.

About an hour later, another pair of scouts got in on the action. At 7:40, Lieutenant Stockton B. Strong and Ensign Charles B. Irvine pushed over from 14,000 feet, diving out of the sun at the *Zuiho.* No antiaircraft fire licked up at them, and the Zeros were caught out of position. Strong and Irvine released their bombs at 1,500 feet, then raced away as the enemy fighters finally came after them. One of the bombs exploded on the flight deck aft. Suddenly a Zero whipped in behind Strong's Dauntless, but rear-seat gunner Clarence Garlow shot it down. Irvine's gunner got another Japanese fighter. Then the two Dauntlesses made a clean getaway, skipping into the clouds ahead of a dozen Zeros. The *Zuiho* was left with a hole 50 feet in diameter in her deck, unable to launch or land planes.

Meanwhile, Japanese scouts had found Kinkaid's carriers, and counterstrikes were already aloft. The first was led by Lieutenant Commander Mamoru Seki of the *Shokaku* and consisted of 22 Aichi dive bombers, 18 Nakajima torpedo planes and 27 Zeros. The second, of similar make-up, followed *Shokaku's* Lieutenant Commander Shigeharu Murata, who had led the torpedo planes at Pearl Harbor and Midway.

"All planes go in!" Seki ordered at 9:10, whereupon his squadrons roared down at the *Hornet,* (the *Enterprise* had slipped into a rain squall). As the Japanese planes entered their dives, four Wildcats that had been flying combat air patrol braved their own ships' antiaircraft fire to send three of the bombers into the sea. Heavy fire from the cruiser and destroyer screen stopped several Japanese planes, but not all. One bomb slammed into the *Hornet's* flight deck. Then Seki, his dive bomber fatally hit, intentionally crashed through her deck, his bombs detonating inside the ship. In short order two torpedoes smacked into her hull, three more bombs exploded on three different levels, and a burning torpedo plane made another suicide crash forward.

The attack was a costly one for the Japanese. U.S. fighters, along with antiaircraft fire from the ships, ran up the total of felled Japanese planes to 25. But the Japanese had scored heavily as well. The *Hornet* was dead in the water, ablaze in several places and without electrical power or radio communications.

Fortunately, the *Hornet* had launched two strikes—54 planes in all—before the attack, while the *Enterprise* had got off a smaller contingent, including eight Wildcats led by Lieutenant Commander James Flatley. En route to their own targets, Flatley's planes exchanged blows with incoming Zeros, knocking down three but losing four fighters and four torpedo planes—nearly half the attack group—in the process.

At about 9:15, Lieutenant Commander William J. "Gus" Widhelm, leading the first wave of 15 Dauntlesses and four Wildcats, sighted a force of Japanese warships stationed as decoys by Nagumo to draw the Americans away from his carriers. When one of Widhelm's pilots asked if they should attack, Gus shot back, "They're only chicken feed. We're looking for carriers." At that moment, a swarm of Zeros fell out of the sun, and one of Widhelm's Dauntlesses broke away to engage them. It

In a painting by combat artist Tom Lea, pilot A. C. Emerson from the carrier Hornet takes aim at one of the scores of Japanese planes that attacked U.S. warships near Santa Cruz on October 26, 1942. Although Emerson's Wildcat was riddled with bullets, he landed it safely.

was promptly gunned down. The rest of the dive bombers maintained formation, their rear-seat gunners punishing several Zeros that eluded the escort of Wildcats. As dogfights with Zeros caused the American fighters to fall behind, Widhelm and Bombing 8 leader Lieutenant James E. Vose pressed on with their squadrons and ran head on into another bevy of Zeros. Bullets from one of the Japanese fighters punctured Widhelm's oil line. As he prepared to ditch, he sighted the enemy carriers—four of them. "Stay in formation, men," he radioed his squadron, then passed the lead to Lieutenant Vose.

They did. At about 9:30, the 11 surviving Dauntlesses peeled off over the big *Shokaku* and, in the face of fearsome bursts of antiaircraft fire, let loose their 1,000-pound bombs. "And did they paste that flattop!" recalled Widhelm, who, along with his gunner, watched the battle from a life raft (they floated for two days before they were were rescued). The Dauntlesses, he said, "swooped in low and laid their eggs in a line, full length along the deck. It was like blasting a ditch to drain a swamp." The strike put the *Shokaku* out of commission, and she would not return to duty for nine months.

But the *Shokaku* was about to get revenge. Murata's strike approached the *Enterprise* at 10:00. In spite of heavy antiaircraft fire, Japanese Vals registered two hits and a near miss on the carrier, starting fires, killing and wounding many men, and damaging a main turbine bearing. Next, the Kates tried their luck, but they were intercepted by a Fighting 10 division led by Lieutenant Stanley W. Vejtasa. Vejtasa himself nailed half a dozen Kates. The other Wildcats and antiaircraft fire took care of several more—including Murata's aircraft—and the *Enterprise* swiveled safely through the torpedoes that were dropped.

By noon, the Battle of the Santa Cruz Islands seemed nearly over. Admiral Nagumo passed command temporarily to Admiral Kakuta and accompanied his stricken carriers as they limped away to the north. Though few Japanese planes were in any condition to fly, Kakuta continued to launch strikes from the undamaged *Zuikaku* and *Junyo*. His

Gunners on board the Hornet fill the sky with antiaircraft fire during the carrier's desperate struggle against Japanese planes off Santa Cruz. Struck by bombs, torpedoes and two disabled enemy aircraft that were used as suicide weapons, the Hornet went to the bottom.

aggressiveness paid off. At 3:15, Japanese torpedo bombers found the wounded *Hornet.* They bored in and scored one hit that opened the *Hornet's* aft engine room to a flood of sea water. Until this moment, it had seemed as if she might be saved, but her situation rapidly became hopeless as she took on a 14-degree list to starboard. Two more bombs that struck later in the afternoon were superfluous; the decision had already been made to abandon ship.

By nightfall, the *Hornet's* surviving crew members—all but 111 of her complement—had transferred to other ships, but the carrier was reluctant to go down and remained afloat and afire even after two U.S. destroyers had pumped nine torpedoes and more than 400 rounds from their 5-inch guns into her hull. At 8:40, Japanese reconnaissance planes illuminated the scene with flares, and the destroyers fled. A few hours later, two Japanese destroyers appeared and with four torpedoes finally sent the *Hornet* to the bottom.

The Americans had held off the Japanese attempt to regain control of Guadalcanal, but at a high price. With the *Saratoga* and *Enterprise* laid up for repairs, the Americans would have not a single battleworthy aircraft carrier in the Pacific for the next two weeks. Fortunately for them, the Japanese flattops had lost so many planes in the Battle of the Santa Cruz Islands that they were unable to exploit this weakness.

The stalemate in the southern Solomons remained unbroken: Guadalcanal's Henderson Field was still held by the Marines, but the Japanese maintained their grip on the rest of the island. In mid-November,

Pilots in the ready room of the U.S. fast carrier Yorktown examine an intelligence map of Marcus Island, target of an American raid on August 31, 1943. The predawn attack caught the enemy by surprise and effectively wiped out Japanese air strength on the island.

Japanese ships in Rabaul harbor maneuver wildly during a raid by planes from the carriers Saratoga and Princeton on November 5, 1943. Air attacks on the enemy stronghold that month helped clear the way for land-based offensives in the southwestern Pacific.

Admiral Yamamoto sent a force of battleships, cruisers and destroyers to level the field with gunfire; it would be his final bid to dislodge the enemy from Guadalcanal. But American warships and planes, some of them flown to Henderson from the crippled *Enterprise,* were expecting a fight and met the Japanese in a fierce engagement later named the Naval Battle of Guadalcanal. At the end of three days' fighting, both sides claimed victory, but the Imperial Navy had not fired a single shot at Henderson Field and had sustained such serious losses—13 ships sunk and nine damaged—that Yamamoto, increasingly reluctant to keep his forces in the area, favored abandoning the island.

It was not until the end of the year, however, that the inexorable attrition of men, aircraft and ships finally persuaded General Hideki Tojo, Japan's Prime Minister, to concede Guadalcanal. During January 1943, the Americans got a pleasant surprise. The Tokyo Express, instead of ferrying reinforcements, carried small groups of men away. Then, in three big movements on the nights of February 2, 4 and 7, the last 11,000 survivors were taken off what the Japanese had come to call the Island of Death.

With Guadalcanal at last secure, the Americans could begin a stepped-up air offensive against Japanese bases on New Georgia and Bougainville in the central and northern Solomons, at Rabaul on New Britain, and at Lae and Salamaua in New Guinea. Alarmed by the

Americans' new potency, Admiral Yamamoto traveled to Rabaul to take personal command of air operations there, shifting some 200 planes from his carriers to various island airfields. During the second week of April, 1943, he flung his aircraft against airfields and shipping around Guadalcanal, Port Moresby, and Milne Bay and Oro Bay on New Guinea. Although the raids caused havoc, they failed to reverse the recent fortunes of war in the South Pacific.

It was Yamamoto's last battle. On April 14, American codebreakers learned the details of an inspection tour he was to make of a Japanese airfield on Bougainville. On April 18, a flight of Army P-38 Lightning twin-engined fighters from Henderson Field intercepted and shot down Yamamoto's plane. His body was later found in the Bougainville jungle by a Japanese search party.

Yamamoto's death was equivalent to a major defeat. Still, he could be replaced, but not the ships that the Imperial Navy had lost—or at least not quickly enough. Although the Japanese had so far managed to hold the United States at bay in the South Pacific, they were clearly losing the more fundamental battle of war production. After Midway, they had cut back on battleship construction in favor of building additional carriers, but the United States was ahead of them, having begun a similar program of shipbuilding two years earlier. Moreover, the United States's superior industrial and technological base enabled it to produce far more ships—and better ones. No fewer than 33 fast carriers of two entirely new designs were on the way: nine 11,000-ton *Independence*-class light carriers built on cruiser hulls, and two dozen 27,100-ton carriers of the *Essex* class.

The *Essex*-class carriers surpassed all their predecessors: They were more maneuverable, they had thicker armor and greater numbers of antiaircraft weapons, and they were equipped with the latest radar and communications equipment. Following the naval tradition of carrying on the names of ships that had succumbed in battle, two of the new *Essex*-class flattops were christened *Yorktown* and *Lexington,* and others would later be named after the *Hornet* and the *Wasp.*

In addition to the *Essexes* and *Independences,* scores of tiny escort carriers (CVEs) averaging 7,800 tons slipped down the ways of U.S. shipyards "as rapidly as a drunk emits burps," wrote one commentator. The CVEs would hunt U-boats in the Atlantic *(pages 123-127)* and later provide close air support for Allied assaults in the Pacific. These new flattops would begin joining the U.S. Pacific Fleet during the summer of 1943, whereas the first of Japan's new carriers would not be ready until the following spring.

The Americans also proved more accomplished than the Japanese in designing aircraft. Early in 1943, the U.S. aircraft industry would begin mass production of the sturdy Curtiss SB2C Helldiver dive bomber as well as the gull-winged Chance Vought F4U Corsair and the Grumman F6F Hellcat, two fighters that would outclass any of their opposition. No

Pilots of the Lexington's Fighter Squadron 16 exult beside one of their F6F Hellcats after foiling an attack by two dozen Japanese planes off Tarawa on November 23, 1943. The Americans downed 17 of the enemy without suffering a single loss.

less than in shipbuilding, American plane makers showed a marked edge over their Japanese counterparts in quantity as well as quality. By the end of the War, the United States would produce 297,000 aircraft for her military forces. Many were sent to Europe and other battlefields around the globe, but the share that went to the Pacific was nearly three times greater than Japan's total wartime production of 32,000 planes.

The seizure of Guadalcanal marked the first step toward the liberation of the Solomons, but until May of 1943 no substantial progress was made toward Rabaul, the operation's ultimate goal. The main reason for the lull was simple—a shortage of aircraft carriers. Admiral Halsey had only the *Saratoga* in the South Pacific; the *Enterprise* had been ordered north to form the nucleus of a new carrier force that would soon commence operations in the Central Pacific. During the summer, Halsey was reluctant to subject his one battle-scarred flattop to the dangers of land-based enemy air strikes. Consequently, American troops were aided in their snail's-pace progress toward Rabaul by land-based aircraft flying from captured Japanese fields or from airstrips bulldozed by Seabees. In October, however, Admiral Nimitz reinforced Halsey by sending him the light carrier *Princeton.* Frederick "Ted" Sherman, promoted to rear admiral after the loss of the *Lexington* in the Coral Sea, assumed command of both flattops and promptly put them to use.

On the morning of November 1, U.S. troops stormed ashore at Bougainville, an island about halfway between Guadalcanal and Rabaul, under air cover from Sherman's flattops and from airfields on neighboring islands. Sherman launched three strikes in two days against Japanese fields at the north end of Bougainville, then headed south to refuel.

On November 4, Halsey learned that the Japanese had one light and seven heavy cruisers anchored at Rabaul—a serious threat to the American beachhead on Bougainville. He ordered Sherman to launch strikes against them, though it meant putting the two carriers within range of land-based air forces. The plan was doubly risky because the flattops would be stripped of their normal fighter protection: All 52 of the carriers' recently arrived Hellcats would be needed to escort the 23 Avengers and 22 Dauntlesses assigned to the mission, for Halsey expected his attacking force to be heavily outnumbered by Rabaul's defenders. To protect the naked American carriers, he ordered land-based fighters from the southern Solomon Islands to fly combat air patrol. What Halsey did not know was that on November 1, Admiral Mineichi Koga, Yamamoto's replacement, had sent 173 carrier aircraft from Truk in the Caroline Islands to reinforce the base at Rabaul.

As it turned out, the reinforcements made no difference to the raid's outcome, because the Japanese were taken by surprise. At 9 a.m. on November 5, Sherman's carriers, which had sneaked up on Rabaul in bad weather, began launching the strike force. Just before 10:30, American bombs and a couple of torpedoes badly damaged four heavy cruisers and inflicted lesser wounds on two light cruisers and one destroyer. As the sky above the harbor filled with plumes of smoke, the carrier pilots pulled out and regrouped for the flight home, dodging antiaircraft fire and fighting through a swarm of Zeros. Of the 97 planes that went out, only five Hellcats, four Avengers and a single Dauntless failed to make it back, though nearly every plane in the flight was peppered with bullet holes. One Hellcat took more than 200 shots but stayed airborne and landed safely.

On the same day that Sherman's task force hit Rabaul, another carrier group arrived in the South Pacific. Admiral Nimitz had dispatched three brand-new carriers, the *Essex, Bunker Hill* and *Independence,* under the command of Rear Admiral Alfred E. Montgomery, as temporary reinforcements for Halsey. On November 11, Halsey threw both teams against Rabaul—Sherman's to strike from the north, Montgomery's from the south. Land-based fighters from New Georgia augmented the carriers' combat air patrol.

The Japanese were ready this time. Zeros intercepted Montgomery's three air groups when they were still 70 miles from the target. Yet some of the Japanese pilots hesitated. As they closed for battle, they executed beautiful passes, guns firing, then went into fancy acrobatics, hoping to lure the Hellcats away from the bombers. Although the American fighters stripped for action by dropping their belly tanks—a Zero collided with one falling tank and exploded—they did not break formation.

In a remarkable sequence of pictures recording the destruction of a Japanese torpedo bomber, sailors hit the deck (1) as the plane attacks their carrier near the Marshall Islands. The attacker passes inside bursting antiaircraft shells (2 and 3), before being struck in one of its fuel tanks. Within seconds, a wing burns away (4). The aircraft loses altitude (5), then—hidden by smoke and flames—falls into the sea (6).

As Rabaul came in sight, antiaircraft fire burst around the Americans in familiar puffs of black smoke. But something new had been added—puffs of white smoke above them, sprouting snowy streamers that fell toward the American planes. Zeros at a higher altitude were dropping phosphorus incendiary bombs in an attempt to ignite the attacking planes. The American pilots dodged them easily. Then the voice of Commander M. P. Bagdanovich, the cigar-chomping skipper of the *Bunker Hill's* Air Group 17, boomed over the radio. "This is Bags," he said. "There's a cruiser down there and a couple more up ahead. Okay, Moe, take it away."

James E. "Moe" Vose, now a lieutenant commander and skipper of Bombing 17, peeled off his squadron's powerful new Helldivers, joined in their first action by Dauntlesses from the *Essex.* Their bombs struck close to the cruiser and right on top of a destroyer that was loading torpedoes. The explosion aboard the destroyer was so violent that its shock waves jarred the planes. The ship sank like a rock. Now Bagdanovich's TBF Avengers swept in to damage another cruiser and a destroyer, while the Hellcats held station until the last attackers had dived and then went in behind them, strafing warships and merchantmen.

As the U.S. pilots pulled out of their attacks, 40 or 50 orbiting Zeros closed in on the vulnerable planes for stern shots. But the Americans quickly regrouped for the flight back. Fighters used the Thach weave, scissoring back and forth over the bombers and torpedo planes in two-plane sections to thwart the Zeros. Many of the Japanese planes were shot down. Finally, about 40 miles out of Rabaul, the Japanese gave up the chase. Eleven American aircraft, far fewer than expected, had been lost in the action. Aboard the *Essex,* the bomber and torpedo pilots, who usually gave the glamor-boy fighter pilots a hard time, now presented them with boxes of candy, cigarettes and cigars, with poems of appreciation attached.

Sherman's and Montgomery's carrier attacks on Rabaul had major consequences. The Japanese withdrew all their cruisers to Truk, never to return. Fully two thirds of the Japanese carrier pilots sent to Rabaul had been killed. The survivors were recalled to Truk, but the carriers there were now virtually useless for some six months, until new pilots could be trained and shipped out. With the air and naval threat from Rabaul neutralized, there was no further need to assault the nearly 100,000 well-supplied Japanese troops entrenched there. Rabaul, once a prime objective of American strategists, would be bypassed and isolated in accordance with the American policy of leapfrogging such offensively impotent targets. Except for the mopping up on nearby islands, the South Pacific had been secured.

Truk, consisting of more than two dozen small islands in a peaceful lagoon, lay square in the path of the main American offensive in the Central Pacific. By the time the operation was ready to get under way in mid-November, 1943, the United States Fifth Fleet, headquartered at

American torpedo planes turn an enemy merchantman into a smoking ruin during a raid on the Japanese anchorage at Kwajalein on December 4, 1943. Six U.S. aircraft carriers launched the attack after reconnaissance photographs revealed a heavy concentration of enemy ships there.

Pearl Harbor and established expressly for pushing the Japanese all the way back to Japan, had 11 aircraft carriers, with more on the way. Each one, rather than forming the nucleus of a single-carrier task force, was assigned to one of four multicarrier task groups. Command of the task groups—collectively designated the Fast Carrier Task Force—went initially to the senior carrier task group commander, Rear Admiral C. A. Pownall. But in January 1944, Rear Admiral Marc Mitscher, who had been in San Diego for the last five months as Commander Fleet Air West Coast, took over as head of the Fast Carrier Task Force. Mitscher's superior as commander of the Fifth Fleet was Vice Admiral Spruance, the victor at Midway.

On the Fast Carrier Task Force's calendar of engagements, Truk was scheduled for mid-February, 1944. Since the preceding November, the carriers had aided in the capture of Japanese strongholds in the Gilbert and Marshall Islands, striking far afield to prevent distant enemy forces from challenging U.S. troops and also close at hand to soften up Japanese defenses before the Americans assaulted the beaches. The first victories in the Central Pacific were Makin and Tarawa atolls in the Gilbert Islands. Then came Kwajalein and Majuro atolls in the Marshalls.

Eniwetok, also in the Marshalls, was next on the agenda, and D-Day was set for February 16. The weak defense of Kwajalein by the Japanese two weeks earlier made it apparent that not all the U.S. carriers

The new Essex-class carrier U.S.S. Lexington, namesake of the famous Lady Lex sunk in 1942, steams into the wind to land planes during maneuvers in March 1944. The 27,100-ton ship was on her way to support the American landings on the northern coast of New Guinea.

would be required for the landing on Eniwetok. Accordingly, Mitscher and Spruance sailed with nine flattops toward Truk, intending to draw out Admiral Koga's fleet, which was believed to be anchored there. Before dawn on February 16 the Americans launched some six dozen Hellcats toward the harbor; bombers and torpedo planes stayed behind. Mitscher hoped that the Hellcats, freed from escort duty, would weaken Japanese opposition in the air and leave Truk vulnerable to the Helldivers and Avengers that would follow throughout the day. This tactic was a new one, and it worked to perfection.

Taken by surprise, the Japanese scrambled about 80 Zeros to meet the Hellcats, but it was no contest: The Americans shot down some 30 Japanese planes, losing only four of their own. By noon, the American fighters were in control of the skies over Truk. One pilot who scored three kills in the dogfighting later voiced memorable praise for his Hellcat. "These Grummans are beautiful planes," said Lieutenant Eugene A. Valencia. "If they could cook, I'd marry one."

With the Zeros knocked out of the air, the American fighters began to machine-gun enemy planes still on the ground. The strafing Hellcats were succeeded by 18 Avengers dropping incendiary bombs on airfields. This phase of the attack destroyed or damaged more than 250 Japanese aircraft. Meanwhile the dive bombers had a field day in the lagoon, sinking more than 41 ships. Most of them, to the disappointment of the Americans, were not warships but merchantmen; except for

A Japanese torpedo bomber races through a storm of antiaircraft fire in a bid to hole the Yorktown—from which this photograph was taken—on April 29, 1944. Gunners on the carrier, which was taking part in a raid on Japan's naval stronghold at Truk Island, downed the plane seconds later.

eight destroyers and three cruisers, Admiral Koga had withdrawn his forces to the security of Palau, 1,200 miles to the west, before Mitscher arrived. All three cruisers and four of the destroyers were sunk.

By noon on February 17, the largest single carrier action so far in the War—and one of the most successful—was over, and Mitscher headed his flattops eastward, in possession of all but 17 of the aircraft he had sent to battle. Of his ships, only the *Intrepid* was damaged. During a weak Japanese counterattack mounted the preceding evening, a Kate had planted a torpedo in her hull near the stern, jamming her rudder and forcing the carrier to withdraw. Mitscher's losses, however, were a small price to pay for the results: Truk would never again harbor the Japanese Combined Fleet. The assault on Eniwetok proceeded on schedule. By February 22, the atoll was secured.

After Eniwetok, the United States Navy thrust westward toward Japan. About halfway to their goal lay the last major obstacle in the

Central Pacific—the Marianas, a graceful arc of islands that the Japanese regarded as practically part of the homeland itself. According to the Imperial Japanese Navy's strategic doctrine, the watery threshold of the Marianas was to be the setting for the decisive battle in which an all-powerful Combined Fleet would crush an enemy leeched of its strength by a war of attrition.

But as the summer of 1944 approached, the prospects for such an outcome were dim. The Combined Fleet had become the weakling, whereas the U.S. Fifth Fleet—continuing to benefit from America's unrivaled industrial capacity—had never been stronger. For the assault on Saipan, the major Japanese stronghold in the Marianas, Admiral Spruance's Fifth Fleet still had Mitscher, vice admiral since March, at the head of a carrier task force comprising 15 fast carriers, nearly 900 aircraft, seven battleships speedy enough to match stride with the carriers, 21 cruisers and 67 destroyers. In addition, the Fifth Fleet's landing forces—almost 130,000 strong—had a shield of eight escort carriers with 200 planes, six battleships, 11 cruisers and a proportionate number of destroyers.

The Japanese fleet, though small, was hardly puny. Admiral Jisaburo Ozawa, who had replaced Nagumo as commander of the Carrier Strike Force in late 1943, now led a Mobile Fleet of nine fast carriers with 450 planes, five battleships, 10 heavy cruisers, two light cruisers and 27 destroyers. Although Ozawa's forces were outnumbered by Mitscher's Fast Carrier Task Force in every category except heavy cruisers, the Japanese admiral had three tactical advantages. First, his carrier planes, because they lacked the extra weight of armor and self-sealing tanks, had a greater range than Mitscher's aircraft. The Japanese planes had a search radius of 560 miles and, assuming a normal expenditure of fuel, they could attack targets up to 400 miles away. The Americans could reconnoiter to a distance of only 350 miles, and generally they could not attack much beyond 200 miles. Second, Ozawa planned to keep the battle within range of land-based planes at Guam in the Marianas and Yap in the western Carolines. Finally, coming from the west, Ozawa faced into the easterly trade wind, which would allow him to launch and recover planes without heading away from his opponent.

However, Ozawa's tactical advantages were largely offset by one major handicap: His carrier pilots were undertrained. Since the previous year, severe fuel shortages and the lack of aircraft had made it impossible for the Imperial Navy to give its fliers the kind of training they had received early in the War. Instead of logging 700 hours of precombat flight time as they once had, pilots flew only 275 hours before being sent into battle. Moreover, new pilots never benefited from the experience acquired by veterans. Unlike the United States, which regularly rotated its pilots temporarily to rear-echelon posts and assigned its most successful ones to training duty, Japan did not take its aviators out of the front line unless they fell ill or were wounded.

The fast carriers sortied from Majuro on June 6, 1944, in advance of the landing force that was to hit Saipan on the 15th. Late the preceding February, Saipan had received a preview of what to expect from Mitscher. He had taken the opportunity afforded by a photoreconnaissance assignment to destroy 168 Japanese aircraft by means of the same tactics he had employed at Truk. To compound the injury, Mitscher's bombers sank several enemy transports and drove others into the lethal arms of American submarines ringing the island. That double attack had cost Japan 45,000 tons of shipping. Now, on June 11, a big Hellcat fighter sweep rained destruction on the island's 150 land-based planes, catching most of them on the ground. "For about two hours," a Japanese sergeant recorded in his diary, "the enemy planes ran amuck and finally left leisurely. All we could do was watch helplessly."

Using submarine reports of warship movements, Spruance calculated that the climactic confrontation of fleets would take place on the 18th or 19th. Over the next few days, tension mounted as the two opposed naval forces extended their feelers and moved ever closer to the impending Battle of the Philippine Sea.

Mitscher sought Spruance's permission for the fast carriers to meet the enemy head on. But in a decision that would spark a great deal of controversy after the battle, the Fifth Fleet commander refused. He saw his mission clearly: It was to ensure the success of the assault on Saipan, already in progress. Spruance would not jeopardize it by detaching the fast carriers, a move that he believed might allow the U.S. forces to be outflanked by Ozawa's forces, whose strength and disposition were not fully known.

Dawn on June 19 found Mitscher's flagship *Lexington* less than 150 miles southwest of Saipan. There was as yet no sign of enemy ships or planes, so, at Spruance's suggestion, Mitscher dispatched some 30 Hellcats to neutralize the Japanese airfield on Guam, where, Spruance reasoned, Ozawa would want to refuel his planes during the approaching battle. At about 8:30, a succession of brisk dogfights broke out in the skies above Guam, but about an hour and a half later the scene of hottest action switched abruptly seaward; enemy carrier-based aircraft had been detected by radar 150 miles away and closing. Just before 10:30 a.m., Mitscher's carriers turned into the wind and began launching fighters to intercept the incoming planes.

Ozawa's 16 Zeros, 45 fighter-bombers and eight torpedo planes were met by hundreds of Hellcats launched from every carrier in the task force. At least 25 of the attackers were shot down during the first skirmish. Then, when the Hellcats wheeled to slash at the 40 or so that pressed on, 16 more plummeted in flames. None reached the carriers, although one dropped a bomb on the battleship *South Dakota,* killing 27 and wounding 23 of her crewmen. Only 24 Japanese planes of this first wave survived. Ozawa's second strike fared even worse, losing 98 of 128 planes.

The Japanese nemesis on that day was Lieutenant Alexander Vraciu,

Vice Admiral Marc Mitscher, one of the most popular U.S. naval leaders, watches takeoffs from the Lexington during the Battle of the Philippine Sea. "His sensible qualities," wrote one of his men, "kept us alive and willing to go any place, provided he led us."

a Hellcat pilot who had downed 13 Japanese planes in previous encounters. Minutes after taking off from his ship, the *Lexington,* Vraciu was mixing it up with ragged formations of Yokosuka D4Y Judy dive bombers. His first victim exploded only 200 feet in front of him. Slipping past the Judy's debris, Vraciu spotted two more of the dive bombers and maneuvered himself behind them. He fired at one, and it began to smoke and dive toward the sea, its tail gunner shooting back relentlessly and ineffectively until the Judy splashed into the water. Flames flickered from the second Judy of the pair as Vraciu pumped short bursts of .50-caliber machine-gun fire into it. The pilot never regained control of his aircraft.

Slightly more than three minutes had elapsed and Vraciu had downed three aircraft, but his morning's work was only half-finished. He shot down two more Judys as the enemy planes approached the pushover point for their dives. Then he dived after a sixth, already making its attack. As Vraciu followed the plane down, antiaircraft fire from his own ships began to burst around him. Then the Judy disintegrated in a bright flash, and Vraciu, seeing no other targets nearby, headed for the *Lexington.*

Ozawa loosed two more strikes, both of which met fates similar to those of the first two. Several of Mitscher's pilots shot down three or more enemy planes; the poorly trained Japanese pilots were simply no

Smoke billows from a seaplane base on the Japanese-occupied island of Saipan during a raid by carrier-based bombers of Task Force 58. The wholesale destruction of Japanese aircraft on the ground paved the way for an invasion by American Marines.

match for them. "Hell," quipped one American pilot during the melee, "this is like an old-time turkey shoot." His opinion was immortalized in the name given to this day of frenetic air battles above the Philippine Sea—the Marianas Turkey Shoot.

It was, in truth, a slaughter. In all, Ozawa lost close to 350 aircraft to the Americans' 30. Nor were aircraft his only losses. The *Taiho,* newest and largest of Japan's carriers, and the veteran *Shokaku* were both sunk by prowling U.S. submarines. On the evening of June 19, Ozawa withdrew to refuel, but the fight had gone out of him. The next day, he began his retreat.

Mitscher gave chase that night and all the next day. At sunset on the 20th, he launched an unprecedented 300-mile strike, fully realizing that many of the 216 planes that participated would have to struggle home on near-empty tanks and land on the carriers after dark, a feat never attempted by most of these pilots before. Mitscher knew that many of the planes would run out of fuel or crash in the landing attempt.

The fliers executed their mission splendidly. Hellcats shot down more of Ozawa's remaining 65 fighters, while Avengers sank the flattop *Hiyo* and Dauntlesses and Helldivers heavily damaged the carriers *Zuikaku, Junyo* and *Chiyoda.* As the planes straggled back, Mitscher flouted a virtually inviolable rule of naval warfare. Ignoring the risk of attack by enemy subs, he ordered the entire task force to be illuminated. Light flooded the flight decks of his carriers. Cruisers bathed the scene in the brilliant bursts of star shells, as destroyers scurried about and retrieved 52 of the 101 fliers who went into the drink.

But six of Ozawa's carriers had eluded destruction to fight again, a fact that did not escape notice back at Pacific Fleet headquarters. In a press conference after the battle, fleet commander Admiral Nimitz and Chief of Naval Operations Admiral King faced the question as to whether their forces had muffed a chance to annihilate a large part of the Japanese fleet. "Admiral Nimitz sat silently thoughtful for many seconds," one war correspondent recorded, "and Admiral King's eyes were closed." Finally, Nimitz answered: "The primary mission of the fleet was to protect the amphibious landings on Saipan and support those landings from the sea. The mission was accomplished."

By August, U.S. ground forces had all but cleared the stubborn—and, at the end, suicidal—Japanese troops from the Marianas. Work soon began on airfields that could handle the long-range B-29 Superfortress strategic bombers that would strike at Japan itself in the fall.

While Spruance and Mitscher were making a clean sweep of the Central Pacific, General Douglas MacArthur's forces in the South Pacific were advancing westward through New Guinea. In a series of crisp amphibious operations along the coast and against offshore islands, MacArthur expelled the Japanese from Hollandia, Wakde, Biak, Noemfoor and Sansapor, and by August 1944 he was in control of all New Guinea. MacArthur's next objective would be the Philippines and, in the fall, the fast carriers would join him there.

Hit during a raid in mid-June, 1944, a Japanese torpedo plane plummets seaward near the escort carrier Kitkun Bay (foreground)

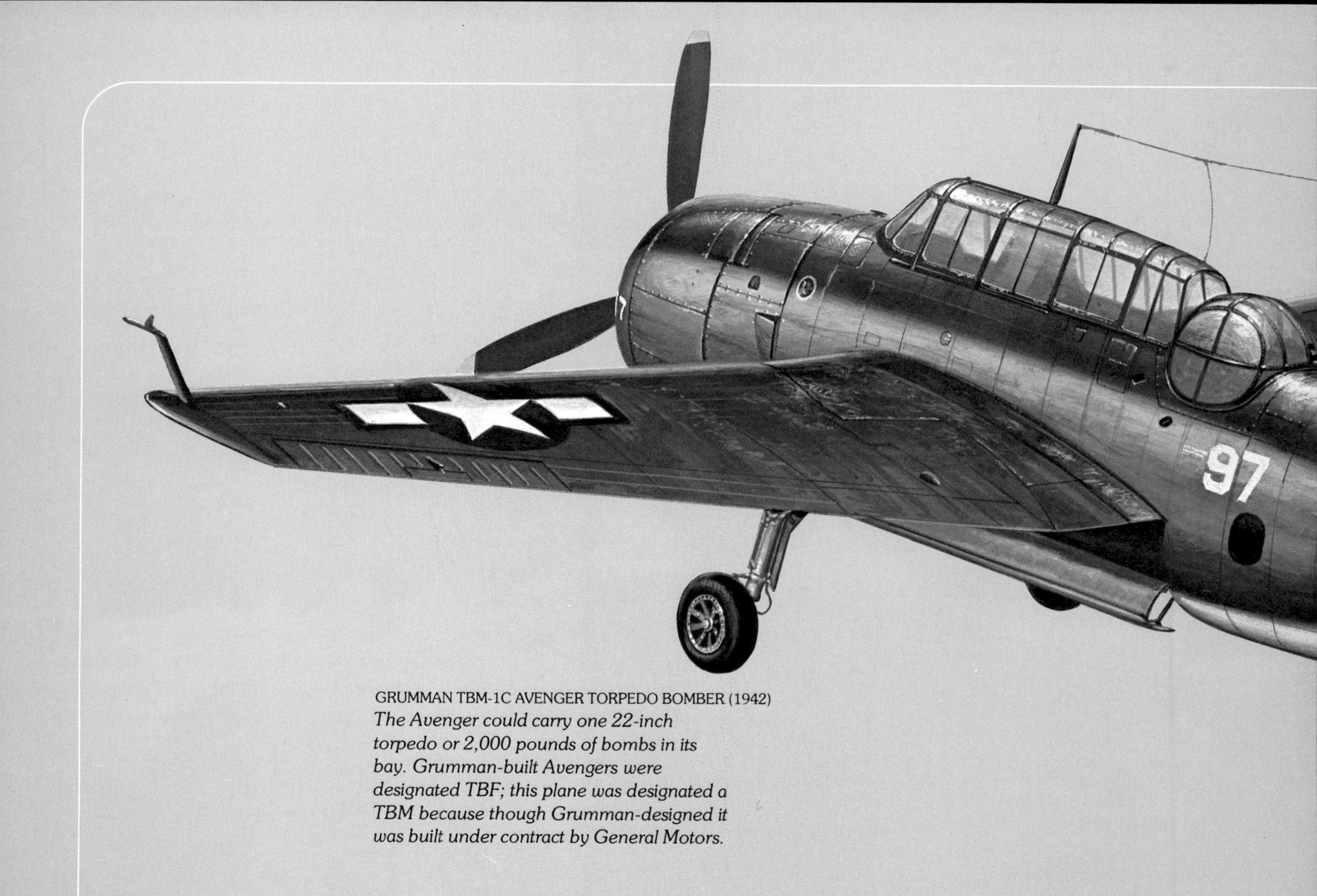

GRUMMAN TBM-1C AVENGER TORPEDO BOMBER (1942)
The Avenger could carry one 22-inch torpedo or 2,000 pounds of bombs in its bay. Grumman-built Avengers were designated TBF; this plane was designated a TBM because though Grumman-designed it was built under contract by General Motors.

Shifts in the aircraft line-up

As the struggle in the Pacific raged on, both America and Japan introduced new, high-performance planes in an effort to gain the upper hand in naval air power. The most important of the second-generation carrier-based aircraft are presented here and on the following pages; the accompanying dates indicate when these particular models entered service.

In the race for more and better planes, the United States soon outdistanced Japan. The Avenger, for instance—a sturdy three-seater Grumman torpedo bomber that replaced the Douglas Devastator—boasted the most diverse armament of any carrier-based aircraft in the War. In addition to its fixed .30- and .50-caliber machine guns, the Avenger could be armed with depth charges, acoustic homing torpedoes, air-to-surface rockets, aerial mines, conventional torpedoes or bombs.

The two Japanese Navy aircraft shown at left and overleaf—a torpedo bomber and a dive bomber—also were great improvements on the warplanes they replaced, but by the time they entered the War a lack of skilled pilots and the overwhelming superiority of America's new Hellcat fighter rendered them virtually ineffective in conventional attacks against the U.S. fleet. In the Battle of the Philippine Sea, for example, the Tenzan torpedo bomber—a much more powerful plane than its predecessor, the Nakajima B5N2 Kate—posed no real threat because it was generally unable to penetrate the phalanx of Hellcats guarding American vessels.

NAKAJIMA B6N2 TENZAN CARRIER ATTACK BOMBER (1944)
Code-named Jill by the Allies, the Tenzan torpedo bomber had an engine that was about 85 per cent more powerful than that of the Kate, the plane it replaced. With a top speed of 299 mph, it was 64 mph faster.

Judy and the Beast

One of America's late entries into the Pacific war was a big disappointment—at least initially. The Curtiss Helldiver dive bomber "offered little improvement" on the SBD Dauntless, said the squadron commander who supervised the new plane's carrier trials.

The prototype, which crashed twice, was extremely unstable. But a contract for 200 Helldivers had been awarded three weeks before the plane's first flight, and labor and parts had already been committed to the project, so the Navy stuck by its choice. Later, after rebuilding the prototype and modifying early models, Curtiss and the Navy were able to correct the aircraft's defects. By the War's end, the much-improved Helldiver had won praise for its performance in several major actions.

Japan's trim new dive bomber, the Yokosuka Suisei, was a faster plane than the Helldiver, but like the Tenzan torpedo bomber, it was unable to get through the newly strengthened shield of American fighters to show its worth.

CURTISS SB2C-1C HELLDIVER DIVE BOMBER (1943)
Dubbed the Beast by its pilots, the Helldiver had a top speed of 273 mph and could carry 2,000 pounds of bombs. The distinctive green spinner indicates that this plane was based on the carrier Yorktown.

YOKOSUKA D4Y1 SUISEI CARRIER BOMBER (1943)
Modeled on Germany's Heinkel 118 V4 dive bomber, the Suisei—code-named Judy by the Americans— was 70 mph faster than the Helldiver but could carry less than half the American plane's payload. In 1945, a specialized version of the Suisei was used as a kamikaze attack plane.

GRUMMAN F6F-5 HELLCAT CARRIER FIGHTER (1944)
This Hellcat from the Princeton has an auxiliary fuel tank slung beneath its fuselage to give it a range of 1,300 miles. Hellcats accounted for nearly 75 per cent of all the U.S. Navy's air-to-air combat victories.

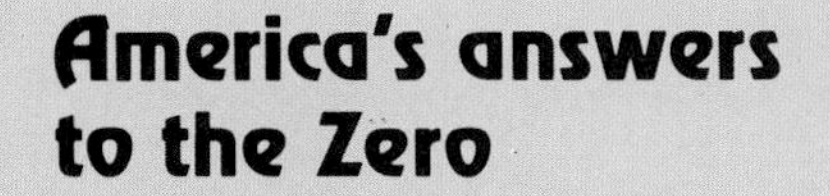

America's answers to the Zero

The F6F Hellcat, said David McCampbell, the U.S. Navy's leading ace, was "the greatest plane of the War." There were other claimants to the title but, beyond dispute, the rugged, 380-mph Grumman fighter was a superb aircraft. Although the Hellcat was less maneuverable than the Zero—which the Japanese Navy had not replaced—its superior armor, speed and high-altitude performance more than compensated.

In flying combat air patrol for the Navy, the Hellcat was eventually joined by an even faster plane, the Chance Vought Corsair. This fighter had at first been assigned to land-based Navy and Marine Corps squadrons, since it tended to bounce on landing; but the problem was corrected, and the Corsair was placed on flattops late in the War, when carrier fighter units were beefed up to counter kamikaze attacks.

Together, the Hellcats and Corsairs overwhelmed the once-fearsome Zeros and reclaimed the Pacific skies, downing a total of 7,295 enemy aircraft.

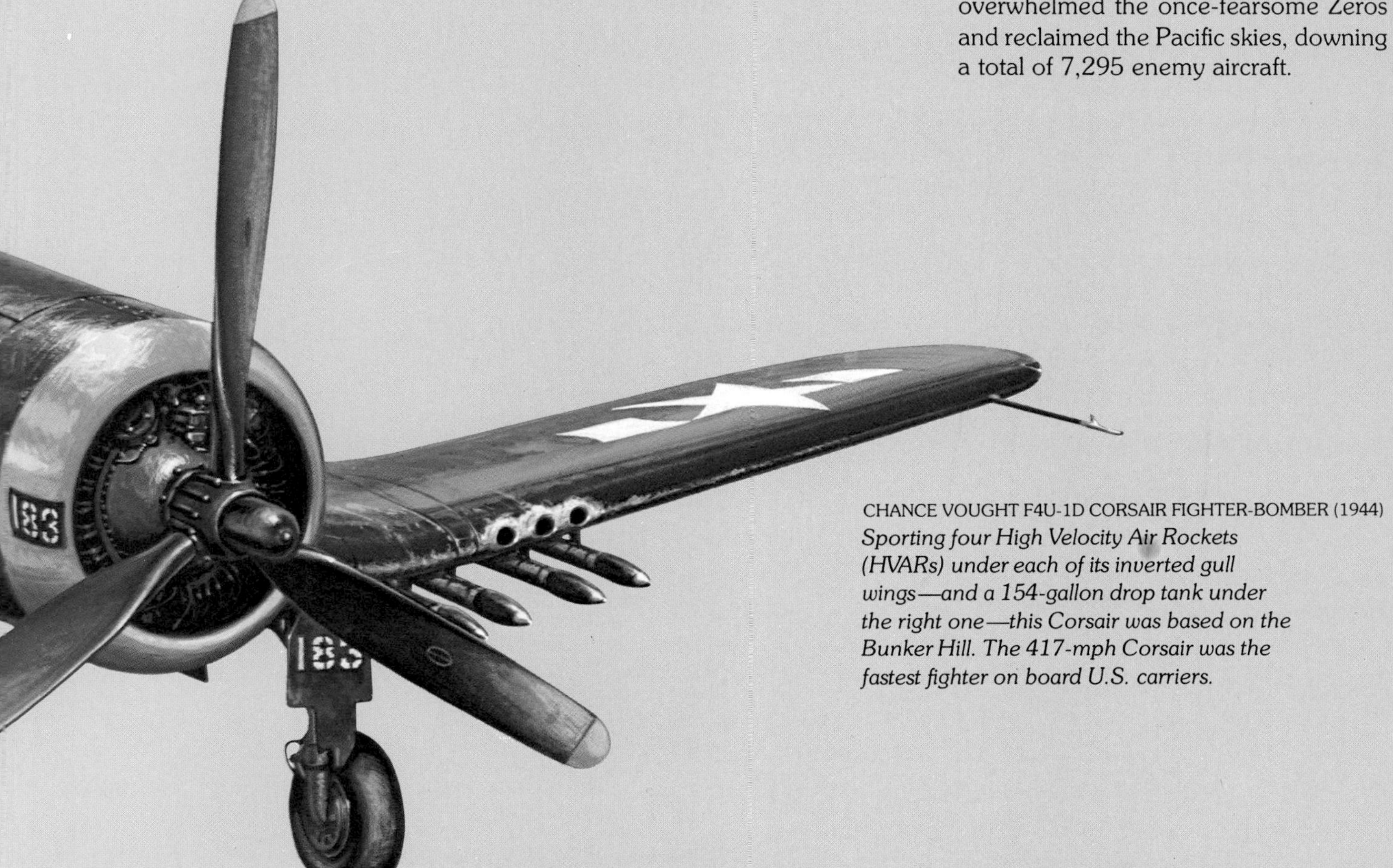

CHANCE VOUGHT F4U-1D CORSAIR FIGHTER-BOMBER (1944)
Sporting four High Velocity Air Rockets (HVARs) under each of its inverted gull wings—and a 154-gallon drop tank under the right one—this Corsair was based on the Bunker Hill. The 417-mph Corsair was the fastest fighter on board U.S. carriers.

5

"We wish for the best place after death"

Shortly before 11 o'clock on the morning of October 25, 1944, Captain F. J. McKenna secured his ship, the escort carrier *St. Lo,* from general quarters. Nothing threatened on the horizon of Leyte Gulf, the body of water in the eastern Philippines that he was patrolling, and his crew, continuously on alert since first light, needed a break. But unknown to McKenna and his men, five Japanese Navy Zeros were rushing toward the *St. Lo* and five other escort carriers in Leyte Gulf. The Zeros flew so near the water that they were detected neither by radar nor by fighters patrolling thousands of feet above. Minutes from the ships, the Japanese planes pulled up sharply to 5,000 feet and then dived into the attack.

The pilots, flying from the Philippine island of Luzon, had an extraordinary assignment. They planned to deliberately smash their planes into the carriers. The first Zero hit the escort carrier *Kitkun Bay,* causing considerable damage. Two others dived on the *Fanshaw Bay,* but antiaircraft fire from the carrier's sharpshooting batteries knocked them both into the sea. The remaining planes screamed down toward the *White Plains.*

It seemed for a moment that the *St. Lo* would come through this bizarre attack without a scratch. Then a trail of oily smoke veered toward the *St. Lo;* one of the Zeros, damaged by gunfire, had changed course.

The *St. Lo* had been under a nautical jinx since the previous month, when the Navy had reclaimed her maiden name, *Midway,* for a new class of aircraft carrier. Old seamen contend that changing a ship's name brings bad luck, and the *St. Lo* was about to receive her full share. The smoking Zero crashed through the flight deck, spilling burning fuel across the hangar deck below. Before the fire could be put out, some of the *St. Lo's* bombs and torpedoes exploded in fireballs that blasted jagged shards of the aft elevator hundreds of feet into the air and heaved entire aircraft into the sea. Little more than half an hour later, she sank, with the loss of about 100 men. Japan's corps of suicide pilots, the kamikazes, had claimed its first enemy ship.

This kamikaze attack was just one encounter in the grandest naval engagement of all time—the Battle of Leyte Gulf. The battle, which involved a greater array of ships than fought in World War I's Battle of Jutland, had been precipitated five days earlier: On October 20 the Americans, capping a four-month string of island-hopping victories that followed the Marianas Turkey Shoot, landed troops on the Philippine

A plummeting kamikaze plane narrowly misses the U.S. escort carrier Sangamon in early May, 1945. During the last year of the War, the Japanese Navy expended many of its remaining aircraft in these suicide missions in a desperate attempt to halt the American fleet.

In a ceremonial send-off, five youthful kamikazes of the Shomu (Sacred and Brave) Squadron share a toast of sake with Vice Admiral Shigeru Fukudome (right), Commander of Japan's First Combined Land-Based Air Force.

island of Leyte. General Douglas MacArthur's long-promised liberation of the Philippines had begun.

The kamikaze raid foreshadowed the kind of war that the carriers would fight in the months to come. There would be no more carrier duels; American flattops would serve as a shield as well as a sword, fending off swarms of suicide-bent Japanese pilots while helping the Army and Marines dislodge tenacious Japanese troops from island fortresses that blocked the Americans' advance toward Japan.

As soon as the Japanese learned that MacArthur's objective was the Philippines, they activated a contingency plan conceived for just such an eventuality. In concept the plan—called *Sho 1,* or "Victory 1"—was simple. First, Japan's aircraft carriers were to keep the American flattops occupied while the rest of the Japanese fleet, numbering 56 combat vessels, routed American warships guarding MacArthur's invasion force. Then the Japanese ships were to destroy the transports carrying ammunition, food and equipment for the American invasion. All well and good—but the American combat force was so strong, numbering more than 200 warships, that a miracle would be necessary for the plan to work, and the leaders of the Japanese Navy knew it. When *Sho 1* was presented to Emperor Hirohito for approval, one Japanese admiral pleaded: "Give us of the Combined Fleet a chance to bloom as flowers of death." A glorious death in a vain attack was a fate preferable to cowering in port.

Even the remotest possibility of punishing the Americans was lost when the Japanese warships failed to act in concert. Instead of arriving in Leyte Gulf simultaneously, they approached haphazardly, allowing Admiral William Halsey, commander of the U.S. Third Fleet, to engage them piecemeal. *Sho 1* became a shambles.

The Japanese aircraft carriers, at least, got into position to fulfill their part of the plan. Vice Admiral Jisaburo Ozawa had set out for Leyte Gulf

Assigned to hurl themselves against the approaching American fleet, Japanese suicide pilots start up their bomb-laden Zeros on a makeshift runway near Manila Bay. About one out of every four kamikazes scored a hit on a U.S. ship.

on October 20, his flag snapping briskly from the mast of the carrier *Zuikaku.* His force, however, was not what it seemed to be. Neither his mighty flagship, which had helped to humble the U.S. Pacific Fleet at Pearl Harbor three years earlier, nor any of the other carriers in Ozawa's retinue had the planes necessary to do battle with the enemy. In October 1944, Japan simply could not muster enough skilled pilots to man her flattops. Almost all of the 108 aircraft aboard Ozawa's ships were merely hitching a ride to their assigned air bases in the Philippines.

In any case, striking power was of little consequence to Ozawa's mission. *Sho 1* called for him not to attack the enemy fleet but to lure the American fast carriers, which were under the command of Vice Admiral Marc Mitscher, away from the Japanese main force of battleships. The Japanese carriers were doomed decoys. It was an ignominious role for such illustrious ships, but they had become expendable: There was little oil to fuel them, and the Americans had advanced so far that they were now within range of Japanese land-based aircraft.

To Ozawa's consternation, he found it surprisingly difficult to attract the enemy carriers. He had expected to encounter American submarines. None were there, either to challenge him or to report his progress. On October 23 he transmitted a long radio message to allow the Americans to get a bearing on his position. That ploy failed, so shortly before noon on the next day he tried another, sending some of his hitchhiking

planes to attack the American carriers. The aircraft bombed from high altitude, caused no damage and retreated with a number of casualties to Luzon. Ozawa had not expected to inflict any serious wounds on Mitscher's force, but he hoped the Americans would deduce that the raid had originated from carriers and would then set out to find him. The stratagem worked; five hours later an American scout tracked down the Japanese ships and reported their position.

Lacking sufficient time to launch a strike before dusk, the Americans had to wait until the next day. Through the early-morning hours, armorers and mechanics clambered over the American planes. The pilots were impatient. For the first time since the Battle of the Philippine Sea they would get to home in on the most enticing targets afloat.

Mitscher launched a dawn search to reestablish Ozawa's exact position, then immediately dispatched strike aircraft in his general direction. The planes were already on the way when the scouts pinpointed the ships, at a little past 7 a.m. At 8 a.m., Mitscher's Helldivers plunged down against Ozawa's carriers. Then a flight of Avengers swept in. Over the next 10 hours, six air strikes loosed bombs and torpedoes against the nearly defenseless Japanese flattops and their escorts. There were few casualties among the Americans and much excitement. One young pilot, upon returning to the *Lexington,* bounded up a ladder to Mitscher's command post in the island and shouted at the taciturn admiral, "I got a hit on a carrier! I got a hit on a carrier!" And he was not alone. At least four Avenger pilots scored on the *Zuikaku* with torpedoes; she sank shortly after 2 p.m., Ozawa having transferred his flag to the cruiser *Oyodo.* The *Zuikaku* had been preceded to the bottom by the carrier *Chitose* and a destroyer, and she was followed later in the afternoon by the carriers *Chiyoda* and *Zuiho.* To achieve these results, the Americans had dispatched 527 sorties and had lost fewer than 20 aircraft.

Ozawa was very nearly a complete success in his role as a decoy. His sole failure lay in not attracting attention to himself sooner than he did. As a result, just hours before he was discovered, American planes sank a Japanese battleship that Ozawa was meant to protect. But the fast-carrier action was the only one of four engagements in the Battle of Leyte Gulf that went according to Japanese plans. In the others, the Imperial Navy was soundly trounced. After three days of fighting, Japan lost a total of four carriers, three battleships (two were sent to the bottom by U.S. battlewagons and destroyers), nine cruisers and eight destroyers. But the American victory did not come cheaply. A lone Japanese Judy hit the fast carrier *Princeton* with two 550-pound bombs that penetrated to the hangar deck and set off six Avengers loaded with torpedoes. The damage from the explosion was so great that the ship had to be scuttled. The U.S. Navy also lost two destroyers, a destroyer escort and two escort carriers—the *St. Lo* and the *Gambier Bay.* The latter ship earned the dubious distinction of being the only American aircraft carrier sunk by gunfire during the War. She was one of six escort

As an approaching Hellcat veers sharply to get out of the way, a Japanese Zero plummets from thick cloud cover and smashes into the escort carrier Suwannee near Leyte Gulf on October 25, 1944. The Suwannee, one of the first targets of a kamikaze strike, was repaired in two hours.

carriers attacked by Japanese battleships and cruisers that slipped up on them after the fast carriers had sped north to engage Ozawa.

The Battle of Leyte Gulf had pulled the teeth of the Japanese fleet, but America's lodgment in the Philippines was by no means secure. MacArthur's troops were encountering stiff resistance ashore, and kamikaze pilots threatened to succeed where the Japanese warships had failed—namely, in bringing the U.S. Navy to its knees.

Kamikaze, meaning "Divine Wind," was an echo from Japan's legendary past. It was the name of a wind god who was said to have sent a typhoon that repulsed a Mongol invasion fleet heading for Japan in the year 1281. Now, nearly seven centuries later, the Divine Wind again became anathema to an invading armada.

What the U.S. Navy did not know was that Japan had no other choice in weapons or tactics. The air battles from the Coral Sea to the Marianas had stripped the nation of its best pilots, and American submarines had sunk so many oil tankers that training flights had been severely curtailed. Many student pilots had no time to learn conventional bombing and torpedo tactics.

Faced with these grim realities, Admiral Takijiro Onishi, the tactician who more than three years earlier had favorably assessed the idea of attacking Pearl Harbor, conceived the extreme measure of using Navy planes to crash-dive into enemy ships. The result was a Kamikaze Corps of young volunteers, glad to have the opportunity to serve in so special a role. "The center of kamikaze is morale," explained Captain Rikihei Inoguchi, an officer who was in charge of kamikaze pilots but did not fly on a suicide mission. "Just prior to the Allied landing in the Philippines we felt as follows: we must give our lives to the Emperor and the nation, that is our inborn feeling. We Japanese base our lives on obedience to Emperor and nation. On the other hand we wish for the best place in death, according to *Bushido.*" (*Bushido* was the ancient warrior code.) One kamikaze pilot had a simpler explanation of his role. "I am nothing," he wrote on the eve of his sacrifice, "but a particle of iron attracted by a magnet—the American aircraft carrier."

The first kamikaze pilots were young aviators chosen for the missions because they were the least experienced fliers and therefore the most expendable. In time, however, the pool of pilots would be drained dry. Then kamikazes would be recruited among university students, given rudimentary flight training and sent into battle, in many cases having logged no more than 30 hours in the cockpit.

As the quality of kamikaze pilots declined, so would the sophistication of their aircraft. During the Battle of Leyte Gulf, the Zero, armed with a 550-pound bomb, was the plane most often flown by kamikazes; its maneuverability gave it the best chance of evading American Hellcats. Later, dive-bombers and twin-engined conventional bombers would also be used. Ultimately, however, trainers would be pressed into service. Though slow and vulnerable, they were inexpensive to build and easy for inexperienced pilots to fly. The Japanese supplemented the trainer's small bombload by packing hand grenades into the cockpit with the pilot, making his weapon as deadly as possible.

The initial kamikaze raid had awakened in Admiral Onishi a new hope for Japan. Only 18 sorties had been flown on October 25, and they had sunk one escort carrier and damaged three others. At that rate, Japan could destroy every American ship in the Pacific with planes to spare. The success of the mission enabled Onishi that very night to persuade Admiral Shigeharu Fukudome, his superior, to use as kamikazes all 500 Navy aircraft based at Manila, on Luzon.

Admiral Halsey's "magnets" were at their most attractive as they sailed in confined waters off Leyte, supporting MacArthur's troops in their struggle for the island. On November 25, some 40 kamikazes attacked the carriers. Two bomb-laden Zeros singled out the *Intrepid,* a hard-luck ship that, aside from having been hit by a kamikaze only a month earlier, had also scraped the locks of the Panama Canal and had been torpedoed during the first Truk strike. Crews of luckier ships gave her the nicknames Decrepid, and Unlucky I.

The *Intrepid's* gunners opened up on the two low-flying attackers in the fervent hope of reversing their ship's ill fortunes. The 5-inch and the 40-millimeter guns knocked down one of the kamikazes some 1,500 yards from the ship. As quickly as the gunners could train their weapons, they began firing at the second plane. At the same time, the carrier's short-range 20-millimeter guns joined in. The Zero kept coming, loosed its bomb, then rammed squarely into the flight deck. The small fires caused by the crashing plane were soon brought under control, but the bomb exploded in a ready room, starting a blaze that killed 32 men in an adjacent compartment.

Billowing smoke acted as a beacon, and a third kamikaze bore in on the *Intrepid.* "For God's sake," shouted the carrier's gunnery officer, "are we the only ship in the ocean?" This Zero poured machine-gun fire into the carrier, released its bomb, then struck the flight deck and slid toward the bow, starting more fires. The bomb went off in the hangar deck, setting it ablaze. Alert damage-control crews saved the *Intrepid,* but she would be out of the War for four months.

The same morning a kamikaze slammed into the carrier *Essex,* killing 15 men, and two suicide planes struck the carrier *Cabot,* leaving 36 dead, large holes in the flight deck and hull, and a severely damaged catapult. The American carriers could not endure such battering indefinitely. "Carriers," remarked one American admiral, "are touchy animals. They're Joe Louis with a glass jaw." Halsey realized that he must somehow give that glass jaw better protection in what promised to be a long and difficult Philippine campaign. So he ordered Mitscher to withdraw the carriers to Ulithi atoll, a forward Navy base some 1,200 miles to the southeast.

At Ulithi, the tactical mind of Jimmy Thach, who was now a commander serving as operations officer for the Fast Carrier Task Force, proved just as keen as when he had invented his weave. He convinced

Hit by U.S. carrier planes in November 1944, a Japanese oil tanker (left) clouds the sky with dense smoke while several cargo vessels lie disabled in Manila harbor. The merchant fleet was carrying supplies from the Dutch East Indies to troops defending the Philippines.

Halsey that the only effective counter to the kamikaze menace was to maintain what Thach called a "big blue blanket."

"I developed a system of combined offense and defense in depth," Thach explained later. Defensive fighters were to patrol as far as 60 miles from the carrier task force. Offensively, the carriers would establish a "three strike system to keep fighter patrols over enemy airfields almost continuously." In daylight, one strike would be orbiting above an enemy airfield, strafing or bombing as necessary to disrupt activity on the ground. Meanwhile, another strike was being readied aboard a carrier and a third was en route to or from the airfield. At nightfall, fighters and torpedo bombers would heckle the airfields with sporadic strafing and bombing to discourage takeoffs. This nonstop assault would make it difficult for the Japanese, said Thach, "to join up in large formations for an attack, in spite of the fact that there were some 6,000 enemy aircraft based within range of our carriers."

The fast carriers tried out Thach's blanket in mid-December as MacArthur's forces stormed ashore at Mindoro, an island in the Philippine chain northwest of Leyte. For three days and nights the carrier planes strafed and bombed Japanese aircraft on the ground and shot down the

Admiral William F. "Bull" Halsey Jr., commander of the U.S. Third Fleet, relaxes aboard his flagship, the New Jersey, in early 1945. In March he was awarded the Distinguished Service Medal for his role in directing carrier support of island conquests in the western Pacific.

few planes that took off from airfields on neighboring Luzon. Reeling under this onslaught, the suicide forces could not launch a strike of any consequence until the third day, when 23 planes took off from a field in northern Luzon. Hellcats from a brand-new carrier, the *Ticonderoga,* intercepted them, shot down 18 and drove off the rest without receiving, said one U.S. pilot, "so much as a bullet hole in return." Not one kamikaze reached the carriers during the entire operation, although suicide planes damaged some of MacArthur's assault craft.

Though not the complete protection that Halsey wished, the big blue blanket had proved its worth and was adopted as the standard tactic for countering kamikazes. But to continue its use, the fast carriers needed more fighters, and soon. Over the next few months, the number of fighter squadrons assigned to Halsey's carriers doubled, reaching more than 70. Several of the new units were Marine Corps squadrons quickly trained to operate their F4U Corsairs from a flight deck and rushed to the fast carriers along with fresh Navy Hellcat squadrons. The Navy pilots' new F6F-5 model of the Grumman fighter was in fact a versatile fighter-bomber that could carry heavy loads of bombs and rockets. It enabled each large carrier to trade in many of its less-flexible Helldivers and Avenger torpedo planes and form a separate Hellcat fighter-bomber squadron designated with the letters VBF.

The fleet also acquired special radar-equipped night fighters and bombers to enable it to maintain around-the-clock protection. By January 1945, when General MacArthur was ready to attack his next objective, Luzon, the fast carriers *Independence* and *Enterprise* had been designated as night carriers, with the specific role of harassing Japanese airfields after dark.

By January 17, General MacArthur had a secure beachhead on Luzon. From then on, the Philippine offensive would be primarily a land campaign, and the Navy was relieved of most of its responsibilities in the islands. Under the command of Admiral Spruance—he replaced Halsey on January 28 in a regular rotation of duties between the two officers—the fleet could proceed with the next items on the Allied agenda: the capture of Iwo Jima and Okinawa.

The two islands guarded the approaches to Japan from the south, and seizing them would set the stage for the invasion of the enemy homeland, anticipated for the autumn of 1945. Iwo Jima, less than 800 miles south of Tokyo, was needed to provide a base for Army fighter escorts and an emergency landing field for long-range B-29 Superfortresses flying from the Marianas; the B-29s had been pounding Japanese cities since November. Okinawa was earmarked not only for airfields but as a forward naval base for the invasion of Kyushu, the southernmost of Japan's home islands and the first that the Americans planned to capture.

By this time, the division of labor among aircraft carriers of the U.S. Navy was well established. In general, the small escort carriers—sometimes called jeep carriers—were assigned to bomb and strafe island beaches and enemy strong points as troops landed and advanced. The fast carriers, though they also participated in this activity, operated on a much longer leash, free to attack far behind the battle of the moment.

The Iwo Jima operation was no exception. On February 16, three days before the landing, Admiral Mitscher lay off Japan with 16 fast carriers and 1,000 aircraft, launching raids on industry and airfields in the Tokyo area. He then headed for Iwo Jima to augment the 11 escort carriers that were softening up the island's beaches for the Marines. In this role, confined as they were to a small area of ocean, the carriers could easily be found by enemy aircraft. And that is what happened late in the afternoon of February 21, two days after the start of the Iwo Jima invasion. Eighteen conventional Japanese bombers and 32 kamikazes attempted to strike American ships off the island. Most of the attackers were shot down or driven off by patrolling fighters, but several got through. Two kamikazes smacked into the escort carrier *Bismarck Sea.* Three hours later she sank. Four other kamikazes and four bombs hit the often-battered *Saratoga.* They did not sink her, but for the third time in the War she had to be withdrawn from action for extensive repairs.

After three more weeks of desperate fighting, the Marines claimed a victory on Iwo Jima, and Admiral Mitscher turned his attention toward the next objective—Okinawa. To prepare for that invasion, the carriers once again steamed for Japan to attack airfields on Kyushu and the Japanese fleet in its home port at Kure. The fleet had not appeared in strength since the Battle of Leyte Gulf, but as the noose tightened around the homeland, the Americans expected the Imperial Navy to put up a fight. With powerful vessels such as the *Yamato,* the largest battleship in the world, the Japanese fleet could still deliver a dangerous sting. The carriers launched strikes against Kyushu and Kure on March 18 and 19. In these attacks, a new weapon made its debut—the 11.75-inch Tiny Tim rocket. Carried under the wings of Avengers, Corsairs and Hellcats, the Tiny Tim was expected to deliver its 500-pound explosive warhead with much greater accuracy than pilots achieved with bombs. But the March 19 raid on Kure was disappointing to the Americans. Although several ships, including the *Yamato* and the aircraft carrier *Amagi,* were hit, damage was superficial.

The difficulty lay not only with the new American weapon's failure to live up to its billing for accuracy, but also with the surprising vigor of the Japanese challenge in the air. Pilots of the U.S. Navy and Marine Corps had become accustomed to encountering few Japanese fighters over a target, and those few were often incompetently flown. The Japanese planes over Kure, however, were not Zeros but a special squadron of 40 new Kawanishi NIK2-J Shiden-kai "George" fighters, designed to match the Hellcat. And the squadron's pilots were not undertrained novices but practiced veterans, including the few remaining aces in the Imperial Navy. These stalwarts waded into the Hellcats and Corsairs as if the clock had been turned back to 1942.

Naval Aviation Pilot First Class Shoichi Sugita, with more than 70 kills

Antiaircraft gunners on the new U.S.S. Hornet hammer away at enemy planes off the Japanese coast in February 1945. Their 40-mm. guns fired 120 rounds a minute and had an effective range of about two miles.

to his credit, flew one of the Shiden-kai fighters that dived on a group of unwary Grummans. His squadronmate Saburo Sakai, grounded because there were not enough of the new planes to go around, watched through binoculars from below. "Sugita plummeted like a stone," observed Sakai. "Coming out of his dive, he rolled in against a Hellcat and snapped out a burst." The blast from Sugita's four cannon set the American fighter's engine ablaze, said Sakai, and the Hellcat "careened wildly through the air, out of control. Sugita rolled away and came out directly behind a second Hellcat, sending his cannon shells into the fuselage and cockpit. The Grumman skidded crazily and plummeted for the ocean." After a third and a fourth kill, Sugita landed with his mates, who had alsc scored well. But they were only 40 against hundreds

An attack by a Japanese dive bomber on March 19, 1945, turns the flight deck of the U.S.S. Franklin into an inferno of flame and flying debris.

of U.S. aircraft, and the Americans managed to damage 17 ships.

At sea, Mitscher's carriers were already launching their second strike of the day toward Kure. But operations were interrupted by a few enemy bombers that slipped under the ships' radar and attacked at about 7 a.m. One headed for the *Wasp* and dropped a bomb that pierced several decks and exploded in a galley, where mess crews were preparing breakfast. The blast killed 101 men and wounded 269.

Another Japanese bomber approached the *Franklin* while she was just beginning to launch her second strike. Only seven or eight planes had taken off when the ship's navigator, Lieutenant Commander Stephen Jurika Jr., heard a voice on the radio. "Enemy plane closing on you. One coming toward you!" The *Franklin's* radar picked it up 12 miles out, as it was arcing up for its final run. The *Franklin's* guns swung around, but their crews could not see the aircraft, which was concealed by a low-level haze. Just then a lookout shouted, "We're going to get it!" Jurika glimpsed two bombs tumbling down from the haze toward fully fueled, fully armed planes spotted on the flight deck for launch.

"There was a tremendous explosion," one Marine pilot recalled; another blast shook the ship a split second later. Both bombs had penetrated to the hangar deck. The first wrecked the forward aircraft elevator. The second explosion ignited 40 aircraft on the hangar deck, blew the after elevator out of its well and touched off the strike aircraft assembled above on the flight deck.

The *Franklin*—Big Ben to her crew—became a blazing hell. Hundreds of men were trapped below as the fires spread rapidly. Father Joseph T. O'Callahan, his breakfast cut short, dived under a table when the first bomb exploded. "This is *it!*" he thought. As shattered glass from broken light fixtures pelted him and his shipmates, the chaplain began reciting the Latin words of the last rites. Then came the voice of an unidentified officer: "To get out, make your way along the starboard passage forward and up to the forecastle."

As O'Callahan stumbled along the passage, he recalled later, "the whole ship quivered in a mighty blast. The boys were thrown to the deck and pitched one against the other." They staggered on, and at last reached refuge on the forecastle deck, just below the flight deck—all except for Father O'Callahan, who had turned aside and headed for the hangar deck when he learned that it had been hit and his ministrations would be needed. But he found it to be a "solid mass of fire. Here and there, like coals of special brilliance, were airplane engines glowing white hot, glaring so intensely that their image hurt the eye and branded the memory forever. No one could live a moment there." The chaplain said a quick prayer for those who lay dead in the flames before him and pressed on to find living men who might benefit from his help.

The sense of desperation extended deeper into the ship, where the engines still rumbled. Trapped by blocked passages, men of the black gang—a name carried over from the era of coal-fired ships, when soot had blackened the stokers—huddled in a mess area and listened to

A pilot dives from his Hellcat's cockpit onto the wing to escape flames that engulfed the plane during a crash landing on the Ticonderoga. As the plane touched down, an auxiliary fuel tank broke loose, struck the spinning propeller and exploded.

Lieutenant Donald Gary, an assistant engineer, reassure them. "I know this ship," he said. "I'll find a way out and I'll be back to get you. I mean that. I'll be back to get you!" And return he did, to lead some 300 men through a maze of ventilation shafts to the flight deck, six decks above.

Not that the flight deck was a haven of safety. The ship's executive officer, Commander Joseph Taylor, watched as Tiny Tim rockets set off by the fire whooshed into random flight. "Some screamed by to starboard, some to port, and some straight up the flight deck. Each time one went off, the fire-fighting crews would instinctively hit the deck."

Like successive earthquakes, explosions continued to shake the *Franklin,* and the ship developed a 13-degree list to starboard. By 10 a.m., she lay dead in the water. When Admiral Mitscher signaled from the *Bunker Hill* that Captain Leslie H. Gehres, skipper of the

Franklin, had his permission to abandon ship, Gehres sent an indignant reply: "Hell, we're still afloat!"

More Japanese planes headed toward the huge, stationary pillar of smoke that marked the crippled carrier's position, but patrolling fighters and fire from the escorts and the *Franklin's* last active 40-millimeter guns shot them all down. At 2 p.m., the cruiser *Pittsburgh* took the *Franklin* in tow. The fire fighters quelled the major fires before sundown, and a few hours after midnight on March 20, the black gang fired up the boilers. As the *Franklin's* speed increased to 12 knots, she cast off the towline and steamed for Ulithi, accompanied by a strong escort. Her dead numbered 724, but 265 of her wounded were saved, and 1,700 men who had been forced by the flames to jump overboard were rescued from the water by other ships. Both Lieutenant Gary and Father O'Callahan received the Medal of Honor. Navy Crosses and lesser citations proliferated among the survivors and the fallen.

As the *Franklin* was struggling to survive her ordeal, other carriers continued to launch strikes against airfields in Japan to reduce the threat of air attack when American forces waded ashore on Okinawa. The raids destroyed more than 500 enemy planes, according to U.S. Navy estimates. The fast carriers then pulled back from Japan to concentrate on Okinawa itself, but not before the kamikazes had one more crack at them. On the afternoon of March 21, forty-eight enemy planes headed for Mitscher's task force. All of them were shot down or driven off by the combat air patrol of 150 Hellcats and Corsairs before they could get near the ships.

Despite its failure, this kamikaze group was more potent than the Americans knew. Sixteen Betty bombers among the attackers carried a new kind of kamikaze device—the *Ohka* (Cherry Blossom) bomb. Called the *Baka* (Foolish) bomb by the U.S. Navy, it was in fact a piloted rocket with a warhead containing more than a ton of explosive. The Cherry Blossom, resembling a 20-foot-long torpedo with stubby wooden wings, was carried beneath its mother plane and could be released as far as 20 miles from an American ship. Its pilot, sitting in a cockpit just aft of the wings, fired his rocket engines after release and, only minutes later, dived on his target at a speed approaching 600 miles per hour. During the Okinawa campaign, *Ohkas* would wreak havoc among destroyers and other ships stationed as radar pickets miles from the fleet. However, none of the missiles struck an aircraft carrier.

But the flattops had already taken a considerable beating in other ways. Like the *Franklin,* the *Wasp* had to be withdrawn for repairs. They were joined by the *Enterprise,* which was wounded in a freak accident: She was hit by antiaircraft shells that fell back on her and exploded. Crews of Mitscher's remaining carriers, especially the pilots, were suffering from fatigue after long days in the air or at battle stations. Fortunately, just when the U.S. carrier fleet most needed help, it was reinforced from an unexpected quarter. Britain, which had been transferring ships from the Atlantic to the Pacific as victory came within reach in

Europe, now put at the disposal of the Americans four aircraft carriers—the *Indomitable, Victorious, Illustrious* and *Indefatigable*—and their support ships. The British flattops joined Mitscher's force off Okinawa.

The U.S. Army hit the Okinawa beaches on April 1, 1945. Planes from 12 escort carriers strafed and bombed ahead of the infantry as the fast carriers blanketed Japanese fields on Okinawa and other islands in the Ryukyu chain, which stretches southwest from Kyushu. Divided into four task groups, the fast carriers retired three or four at a time every fourth day to refuel and to replenish stores of food and munitions, a pattern that would be followed until Okinawa was conquered.

Primarily because of the successful American raids on kamikaze airfields in Japan a couple of weeks earlier, the Divine Wind defended Okinawa only sporadically until April 6. But on that date it blew with gale force. For the first time, Japan's Army and Navy combined their kamikaze efforts in *kikusui*—"floating chrysanthemums"—enormous swarms of suicide aircraft attacking day and night.

To inaugurate the *kikusui* campaign, the Japanese Army and Navy assembled 699 aircraft—355 of them kamikazes, the rest fighters and bombers, some carrying *Ohka* bombs—in what would prove to be the largest kamikaze operation of the entire war. During the two days that the attack lasted, Mitscher's Hellcats and Corsairs shot down more than 200 enemy planes; others were destroyed by ships' batteries. Many kamikazes got through. Nonetheless, only one carrier, the *Hancock,* was hit, and she did not sink. The destroyers suffered most; three were sunk and eight sustained major damage. A landing craft was sunk, the battleship *Maryland* suffered 53 casualties from one hit and 10 smaller ships were also damaged or sunk.

As carrier clashed with kamikaze, word came from the submarines *Threadfin* and *Hackleback,* on patrol off the Bungo Strait exit from Japan's Inland Sea, that several unidentified Japanese warships were steaming in a southerly direction. Since the Battle of Leyte Gulf, the Imperial Navy's capital ships had remained in port. Yet it was unthinkable that so grand a battleship as the *Yamato* should make no effort to save Japan or should fall into enemy hands. On April 6, accompanied by the cruiser *Yahagi* and an escort of eight destroyers, the *Yamato* had weighed anchor to attack American ships in Hagushi roadstead off Okinawa. The Japanese knew that the *Yamato* could not survive the mission; she loaded only enough fuel to enable her to reach Okinawa, not enough to return.

Upon receiving the submarines' reports, Admiral Mitscher deployed 12 of his fast carriers to intercept the enemy warships. At 8:23 a.m. on April 7, a scout from the *Essex* sighted the Japanese vessels, and at 10 o'clock the first of hundreds of planes that would be launched that day took off to attack the *Yamato* and her escort.

Low-hanging clouds, rain squalls and mist forced American dive bombers to make low-level attacks, inherently less effective than their usual attacks from an altitude of 12,000 feet. Nevertheless, Helldivers

Ablaze following attacks by American carrier-based planes on April 7, 1945, the superbattleship Yamato struggles toward Okinawa as a bomb bursts off her port side. The mammoth ship—pride of the Japanese Navy—sank later that day after being hit by five bombs and 10 torpedoes.

from the *Bennington* scored two hits near the *Yamato's* mainmast at 12:41 p.m. Four minutes later, an Avenger from the same carrier torpedoed the battleship on the port side near the bow. The *Yamato* defended herself with a storm of antiaircraft fire. Every weapon aboard, from her immense 18-inch rifles to the smallest machine guns, blasted away at the American planes—but with little effect. During the preceding five months, while the *Yamato* had been tied up in port, her gunners had been deprived of the opportunity to hone their skills on live targets, and now they were paying the price.

The *Yamato* was under almost continuous air attack for more than an hour. On the bridge, Ensign Mitsuru Yoshida watched in horror as Avengers planted three more torpedoes in the port side, then raked antiaircraft-gun crews with machine-gun fire. "That these pilots repeated their attacks with such accuracy and coolness," he said later, "was a sheer display of the unfathomable, undreamed-of strength of our foes!"

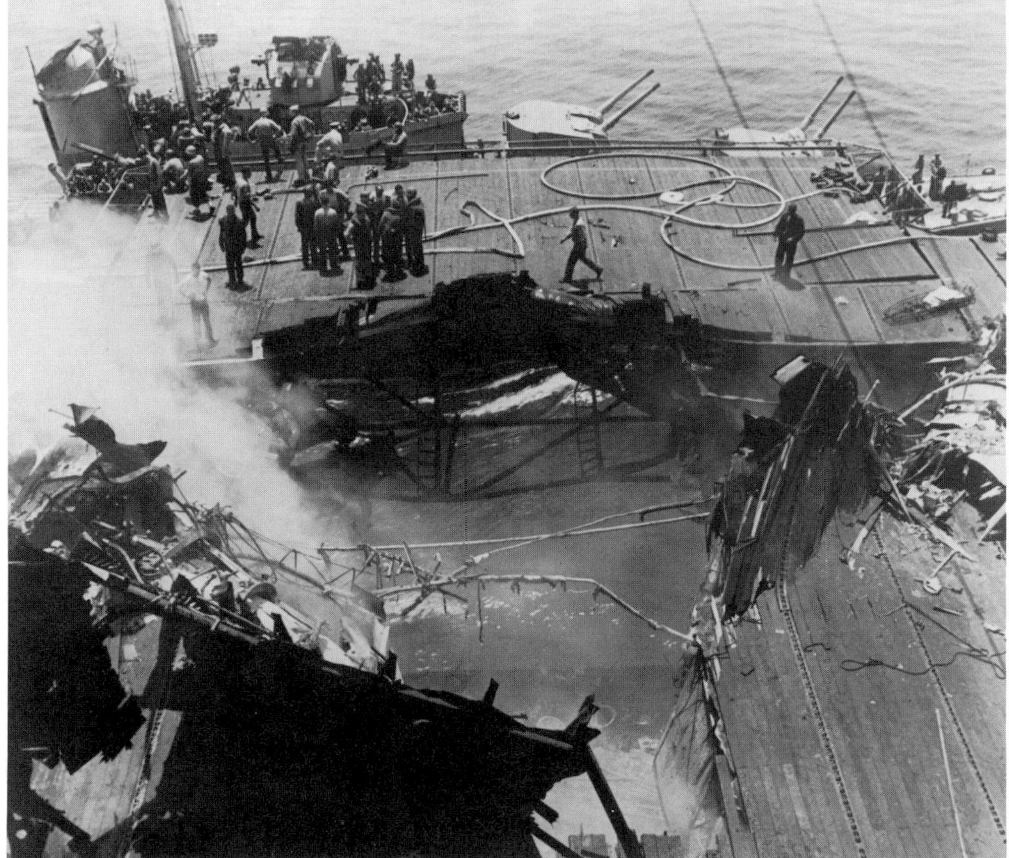

Crewmen aboard the Bunker Hill struggle to douse flames (top) that erupted after the carrier took direct hits by two kamikaze planes on May 11, 1945. A bomb dropped by the second plane cratered the ship's deck (bottom), but the Bunker Hill managed to stay afloat.

The port side of the ship was taking a savage beating. After two more torpedo hits, the *Yamato* developed a slight list; it could not be corrected by counterflooding, because many damage-control personnel had been killed or wounded. Smoke rose from the great battleship, and she gradually began to lose speed. A damaged rudder held her in a lazy turn to port. The American aircraft kept coming, wave upon wave of them, scoring hit after hit. "From near the funnel," recalled Ensign Yoshida, "black smoke was rising in great puffs. There was a sudden increase in our list, and speed fell off to only seven knots! Now we were easy prey to the planes. As though awaiting this moment, the enemy came plunging through the clouds to deliver the *coup de grâce.*" As his captain shouted "Hold on, men!" Yoshida lay down on the deck of the bridge; "I braced myself to withstand the shocks!"

The planes that Yoshida saw were six *Yorktown* Avengers commanded by Lieutenant Thomas Stetson. One of the squadron's rear-seat gunners, Harvey Ewing, held his breath as he neared the ship. "I could see bursts of antiaircraft fire all around the plane as we made the run," he said, "and to say I was scared would be an understatement. We dropped the fish and pulled up on one wing over the *Yamato* and seemed to hang there for minutes as the ship was firing every gun it had, including its 18-inch rifles, at the planes following us in."

At least four torpedoes found their mark. "Great columns of water," Yoshida said, "suddenly rose high into the air on the port side amidships." As the *Yamato* shuddered from the explosions, the sea cascaded into the fresh holes in her side. "The horizon seemed to take on a mad new angle. Dark waves splattered and reached for us as the stricken ship heeled to the incredible list of 80 degrees!" The *Yamato* turned turtle and went under at 2:23 p.m. Yoshida heard "the blast, rumble and shock of compartments bursting from air pressure and exploding magazines already submerged." He was one of only 269 survivors of the *Yamato's* complement of 2,767.

The battleship had plenty of company on the ocean floor that afternoon. The cruiser *Yahagi* and four of the destroyers that had escorted the *Yamato* into battle also escorted her to the bottom. The remaining four destroyers limped back to Japan, having sustained varying degrees of damage. Almost 3,700 Japanese officers and men were killed, at a cost to Admiral Mitscher of only 10 aircraft. If the story of the shift of power at sea from once-mighty dreadnoughts to aircraft carriers needed a final chapter, it was written that afternoon as the *Yamato* went down.

After the excitement of the sinking of the world's largest battleship, Okinawa became a battle of attrition for the U.S. carriers. The *kikusui* attack of April 6 and 7 established a kamikaze pattern. Three more of the mass assaults occurred during April, four in May and two in June. Japanese resistance ashore, suddenly stiffer, kept the United States Army at bay and Mitscher's task force tied to the island, unable to evade kamikaze attacks. Though the big blue blanket was spread round the clock to protect the ships from the *kikusui* onslaughts, not every suicide plane could be fended off. The steel decks of the British flattops proved superior to the Americans' wooden ones in shielding the vitals of a ship. When the H.M.S. *Indefatigable* took a kamikaze squarely on her flight deck, the damage was minimal—a three-inch dent in the armor plating. When another plunged through the deck of the *Intrepid,* the Unlucky I had to return to the United States for major repairs.

The repeated attacks wore down Mitscher's pilots and crews. The general sentiment was expressed in a message to Vice Admiral Joseph J. "Jocko" Clark, one of Mitscher's task group commanders. "See Hebrews 13, verse 8," signaled the commander of the group's screen of antiaircraft ships. Clark chuckled as he read the passage in the Bible: "Jesus Christ, the same yesterday, and today, and forever." Clark circulated the message to his ships, adding, "No irreverence intended."

Although the *kikusui* attacks continued, the number of kamikazes involved gradually diminished—185 on the 12th and 13th of April, 110 on May 27 and 29 and, in the last such effort, only 45 on June 21 and 22. Even so, a total of 1,465 Japanese Army and Navy aircraft flown by kamikaze pilots had been dispatched to Okinawa between April and June. They had sunk 26 American ships and damaged 164 others, including Mitscher's flagship, the *Bunker Hill,* which was knocked out of the War. Coincidental with the final *kikusui* raid in June, organized Japanese resistance on Okinawa ended. Long before then, however, U.S. Army and Marine Corps fighters operating from captured air bases on Okinawa had begun to assume much of the carriers' burden of defending the troops ashore.

The next item on the fast carriers' agenda was to prepare for what promised to be the toughest fight of all—the invasion of the Japanese homeland, scheduled for November 1. It never came to pass; Japan's national life was already almost at an end. B-29s flying from the Marianas were methodically demolishing Japanese cities and industry, and Allied submarine operations and mines dropped from aircraft had brought shipping to a complete halt. The country's economy was at a standstill, and the imperial armed forces were husbanding what little strength they had left to meet the invasion; not a single Japanese fighter took to the air to try to fend off air raids launched against Tokyo and other land targets by the fast carriers during July. Then, on August 6, 1945, a B-29 dropped an atomic bomb on Hiroshima; three days later the devastation was duplicated at Nagasaki. The terrible new weapon hastened the inevitable. Japan capitulated on the 15th.

On August 11, just two days after Nagasaki had been bombed, Admiral Marc Mitscher issued a press release in his new capacity as head of naval aviation in Washington, D.C. He was careful to acknowledge the indispensable contributions to the war against Japan by the rest of the Navy, Army troops, Marines and land-based air forces. But he left no doubt—and students of warfare agreed—that the starring role had been played by aircraft carriers. "Japan is beaten," asserted Mitscher in the release, "and carrier supremacy defeated her."

Decked with streamers and balloons to celebrate America's

victory over Japan, the U.S.S. Yorktown steams into San Francisco Bay in 1945 while crewmen crowd her flight deck for a first glimpse of home.

Acknowledgments

The index for this book was prepared by Gale Linck Partoyan. For their help with the preparation of this book, the editors also wish to thank: **In France:** Paris—André Bénard, Odile Benoist, Elisabeth Bonhomme, Alain Degardin, Georges Delaleau, Gilbert Deloizy, Yvan Kayser, Général Pierre Lissarague, Director, Jean-Yves Lorent, Stéphane Nicolaou, Général Roger de Ruffray, Deputy Director, Colonel Pierre Willefert, Curator, Musée de l'Air; Claude Bellarbre, Jacques Chantriot, Marjolaine Matikhine, Director for Historical Studies, Catherine Touny, Musée de la Marine. **In Great Britain:** Alton, Hampshire—M. H. Brice; Hendon—R. Simpson and R. W. Mack, Royal Air Force Museum; Lee-on-Solent—Laurence Bagley; London—J. O. Simmonds, J. Wood, E. Hine, M. Willis, Imperial War Museum; Marjorie Willis, BBC Hulton Picture Library; E. Moore, *Illustrated London News;* R. Chesneau, Conway Maritime Press; Yeovilton, Somerset—Lieutenant Commander L. A. Cox, Fleet Air Arm Museum. **In Italy:** Rome—Contessa Maria Fede Caproni, Museo Aeronautico Caproni di Taliedo; Admiral Massimiliano Marandino, Director, Stato Maggiore Della Marine, Ufficio Storico. **In Japan:** Atsugi—General Minoru Genda; Fuchu—Hideki Shingo; Higashi-Murayama—Kaneo Fukuchi; Kamakura—Motoyoshi Hori; Kiyose—Hitoshi Yamauchi; Tokyo—Masataka Chihaya, Takashi Iwata, Suguru Mitsumura, Toshio Morimatsu, Masao Murata, Fumio Nishimura, Tadashi Nozawa, Kazuo Takasaki, Mannosuke Toda, Keiichi Yoshino; Tsu—Wataru Yoshikawa; Yokohama—Shizuo Fukui. **In the United States:** Washington, D.C.—John M. Elliott; Don Montgomery, Defense Audio Visual Agency; Philip Edwards, Robert C. Mikesh, Karl P. Suthard, Glenn Sweeting, National Air and Space Museum; Jim Trimble, Paul White, National Archives; John C. Reilly Jr., Michael Walker, Naval Historical Center; Colonel Keisuke Yoshida, Embassy of Japan; New York—James T. Bryan, U.S.S. *Yorktown* CV-10 Association; Colonel John R. Elting, U.S.A. (Ret.); Dick Taylor, United Press International; Pennsylvania—Lieutenant Commander Don Hamblin, U.S.N. (Ret.); Texas—Tom Lea; Virginia—Lou Casey.

Picture credits

The sources for the illustrations in this book are shown below. Credits from left to right are separated by semicolons; from top to bottom they are separated by dashes.
Endpaper (and cover detail, regular edition): Painting by R. G. Smith. 6, 7: U.S. Naval Academy. 8, 9: U.S. Naval Academy; U.S. Navy (3). 10-15: Imperial War Museum, London. 16, 17: National Archives (Nos. 80-G-416312 and 80-G-416300); Culver Pictures. 18, 19: From the collection of Shizuo Fukui, Yokohama—UPI; photo by Rudy Arnold. 20, 21: U.S. Navy. 22, 23: Imperial War Museum, London. 24: BBC Hulton Picture Library, London. 25-31: Imperial War Museum, London. 33, 34: National Archives (Nos. 80-G-460873 and 80-G-451356). 36: Painting by Yukihiko Yasuda, courtesy Tokyo University of Fine Arts. 37: Courtesy General Minoru Genda, Atsugi, Japan. 39, 40: Motoyoshi Hori, Kamakura, Japan. 41: Hideki Shingo, Fuchi, Japan. 42: Popperfoto, London—Derek Bayes, © painting by Laurence Bagley, courtesy R.N.A.S., Yeovilton (Ward Room). 45: Mannosuke Toda, Tokyo. 46-49: U.S. Navy. 50-59: Mannosuke Toda, Tokyo. 60, 61: Kaneo Fukuchi, Higashi-Murayama, Japan. 62, 63: Map by Frederic F. Bigio from B-C Graphics. 64: National Archives (No. 80-G-64834). 65: Drawing by George Snowden. 67: Harris and Ewing Photos. 70: Map by Frederic F. Bigio from B-C Graphics. 71: National Archives (Nos. 80-G-17024 and 80-G-17015). 72: Drawing by Frederic F. Bigio from B-C Graphics. 73-75: National Archives (Nos. 80-G-16802 and 80-G-7398). 76-81: Drawings by John Amendola. 82, 83: U.S. Navy. 85: National Archives (No. 80-G-7133). 86, 87: Peter Stackpole for *Life.* 90: Painting by William Reynolds. 91-95: National Archives (Nos. 80-G-17678, 80-G-701845, 80-G-701850, 80-G-701852, 80-G-701868, 80-G-701898 and 80-G-701859). 98, 99: UPI—U.S. Navy. 100-101: J. R. Eyerman for *Life.* 102, 103: J. R. Eyerman for *Life* (3)—Johnny Florea for *Life;* National Archives (No. 80-G-474667). 104, 105: National Archives; J. R. Eyerman for *Life;* National Archives (Nos. 80-G-471229 and 80-G-470195). 106, 107: U.S. Navy; National Archives (No. 80-G-418194). 108, 109: J. R. Eyerman for *Life*—National Archives (Nos. 80-G-470992 and 80-G-471200). 110-111: National Archives (Nos. 80-G-747693 and 80-G-14376); U.S. Navy. 112, 113: Culver Pictures; National Archives (Nos. 80-G-417636 and 80-G-322077). 114, 115: Courtesy Edgar E. Stebbins. 116: Courtesy *Maru* Monthly Magazine, Tokyo. 118: National Archives (No. 80-G-62431). 119: Drawings by Frederic F. Bigio from B-C Graphics. 121: National Archives (No. 80-G-418212). 123: Courtesy Vice Admiral A. B. Vosseller, U.S.N., (Ret.). 124: Courtesy Vice Admiral A. B. Vosseller, U.S.N., (Ret.) (2); National Archives (No. 80-G-68693). 126, 127: National Archives (No. 80-G-68695). 128: Painting by Tom Lea, courtesy Chief of Military History, U.S. Naval Photographic Center. 129: Painting by Tom Lea, courtesy U.S. Army. 130, 131: National Archives (Nos. 80-G-474630 and 80-G-89095). 133: Culver Pictures. 134, 135: UPI. 136, 137: National Archives (Nos. 80-G-476248 and 80-G-217772). 138: UPI. 140: J. R. Eyerman for *Life.* 141: W. Eugene Smith for *Life.* 142, 143: National Archives (No. 80-G-238363). 144-149: Drawings by John Amendola. 150: National Archives (No. 80-G-700580). 152, 153: Mainichi Press, Tokyo. 154-159: U.S. Navy. 161-163: National Archives (Nos. 80-G-413915 and 80-G-273900). 164-167: UPI. 168: U.S. Navy. 170, 171: National Archives (No. 80-G-376521).

Bibliography

Books

Agawa, Hiroyuki, *The Reluctant Admiral: Yamamoto and the Imperial Navy.* Kodansha International, 1979.

Belote, James H., and William M. Belote, *Titans of the Seas: The Development and Operations of Japanese and American Carrier Task Forces During World War II.* Harper & Row, 1975.

Brown, David, *Aircraft Carriers.* Arco, 1977.

Brown, Eric, *Wings of the Navy: Flying Allied Carrier Aircraft of World War Two.* London: Jane's, 1980.

Collier, Basil, *Japanese Aircraft of World War II.* Mayflower Books, 1979.

Dull, Paul S., *A Battle History of The Imperial Japanese Navy (1941-1945).* Naval Institute Press, 1978.

Falk, Stanley L., *Decision at Leyte.* W. W. Norton & Company, 1962.

Fetridge, William Harrison, ed., *The Navy Reader.* Books for Libraries Press, Reprinted 1971.

Francillon, René J.:
Japanese Carrier Air Groups 1941-1945. London: Osprey, 1979.
U.S. Navy Carrier Air Groups Pacific 1941-1945. London: Osprey, 1978.

Frank, Pat, and Joseph D. Harrington, *Rendezvous at Midway.* John Day, 1967.

Friedman, Norman:
Carrier Air Power. London: Conway Maritime Press, 1981.
USS Yorktown. Leeward Publications, 1977.

Fuchida, Mitsuo, *Midway.* Naval Institute Press, 1955.

Gay, George, *Sole Survivor: The Battle of Midway and Its Effects on His Life.* George H. Gay, 1979.

Green, William, *Famous Bombers of the Second World War.* Doubleday, 1960.

Griffin, Alexander R., *A Ship to Remember.* Howell, Soskin, 1943.

Halsey, William F., and J. Bryan III, *Admiral Halsey's Story.* Da Capo Press, 1976.

Hezlet, Sir Arthur, *Aircraft and Sea Power.* Stein and Day, 1970.

Inoguchi, Rikihei, and Tadashi Nakajima, *The Divine Wind.* Naval Institute Press, 1958.

Ito, Masanori, *The End of the Imperial Japanese Navy.* London: Weidenfeld and Nicolson, 1956.

Jensen, Oliver, *Carrier War.* Simon and Schuster, 1945.

Jentschura, Hansgeorg, Dieter Jung and Peter Mickel, *Warships of the Imperial Japanese Navy, 1869-1945.* Naval Institute Press, 1977.

Johnson, Stanley:
The Grim Reapers. E. P. Dutton, 1943.
Queen of the Flat-Tops: The U.S.S. Lexington and the Coral Sea Battle. E. P. Dutton, 1942.

Karig, Walter:
Battle Report: The Atlantic War. Farrar & Rinehart, 1946.
Battle Report: Pacific War: Middle Phase. Rinehart, 1947.
Battle Report: Victory in the Pacific. Rinehart, 1949.

Kemp, Peter K., *Fleet Air Arm.* London: Herbert Jenkins, 1954.

Lord, Walter:
Day of Infamy. Henry Holt, 1957.
Incredible Victory. Harper & Row, 1957.

MacDonald, Scot, *Evolution of Aircraft Carriers.* U.S. Government Printing Office, 1964.

Marder, Arthur J., *From the Dreadnought to Scapa Flow,* Vols. 3 and 4. London: Oxford University Press, 1969, 1978.

Melhorn, Charles M., *Two-Block Fox.* Naval Institute Press, 1974.

Mikesh, Robert C., *Zero Fighter.* Crown, 1981.

Miller, John, Jr., *Guadalcanal: The First Offensive.* Department of the Army, 1949.

Morison, Samuel Eliot
History of United States Naval Operations in World War II:
Vol. 3, *The Rising Sun in the Pacific.* Little, Brown, 1948.
Vol. 4, *Coral Sea, Midway and Submarine Actions, May 1942-August 1942.* Little, Brown, 1949.
Vol. 5, *The Struggle for Guadalcanal, August 1942-February 1943.* Little, Brown, 1949.
Vol. 8, *New Guinea and the Marianas, March 1944-August 1944.* Little, Brown, 1953.
Vol. 12, *Leyte, June 1944-January 1945.* Little, Brown, 1958.
Vol. 14, *Victory in the Pacific, 1945.* Little, Brown, 1960.
The Two-Ocean War. Little, Brown, 1963.

Naval Aircraft. Chartwell Books, Inc., London: Phoebus, 1977.

O'Callahan, Joseph, *I Was Chaplain on the Franklin.* Macmillan, 1956.

Okumiya, Masatake, and Jiro Horikoshi, *Zero!* E. P. Dutton, 1956.

Olds, Robert, *Helldiver Squadron.* Dodd, Mead, 1944.

Polmar, Norman, *Aircraft Carriers: A Graphic History of Carrier Aviation and Its Influence on World Events.* Doubleday, 1969.

Potter, E. B., *Nimitz.* Naval Institute Press, 1976.

Pratt, Fletcher, *The Navy Has Wings.* Harper & Brothers, 1943.

Reynolds, Clark G.:
Command of the Sea: A History and Strategy of Maritime Empires. William Morrow, 1974.
The Fast Carriers: The Forging of an Air Navy. Robert E. Krieger, 1978.

Reynolds, Clark G., and E. T. Stover, *The Saga of Smokey Stover.* Tradd Street Press, 1978.

Roscoe, Theodore, *On the Seas and in the Skies: A History of the U.S. Navy's Air Power.* Hawthorn Books, 1970.

Sakai, Saburo, Martin Caidin and Fred Saito, *Samurai!* Bantam Books, 1978.

Schofield, B. B., *The Attack on Taranto.* Naval Institute Press, 1973.

Skiera, Joseph A., *Aircraft Carriers in Peace and War.* Franklin Watts, 1965.

Smith, Myron J., Jr., *World War II at Sea:* Vols. 2 and 3. Scarecrow Press, 1976.

Stafford, Edward P., *The Big E: The Story of the USS Enterprise.* Random House, 1962.

Steichen, Edward, *The Blue Ghost.* Harcourt, Brace and Company, 1947.

Taylor, Theodore, *The Magnificent Mitscher.* W. W. Norton, 1954.

Terzibaschitsch, Stefan, *Aircraft Carriers of the U.S. Navy.* Mayflower Books, 1980.

Tillman, Barrett:
Avenger at War. Charles Scribner's Sons, 1980.
Corsair, the F4U in World War II and Korea. Naval Institute Press, 1979.
The Dauntless Dive Bomber of World War Two. Naval Institute Press, 1976.
Hellcat: The F6F in World War II. Naval Institute Press, 1979.

Toliver, Raymond F., and Trevor J. Constable, *Fighter Aces of the U.S.A.* Aero, 1979.

Van Deurs, George:
Anchors in the Sky. Presidio Press, 1978.
Wings for the Fleet. Naval Institute Press, 1966.

Whitehouse, Arch, *Squadrons of the Sea.* Doubleday, 1962.

Wragg, David, *Wings Over the Sea: A History of Naval Aviation.* Arco, 1979.

Young, Desmond, *Rutland of Jutland.* London: Cassell & Company, 1963.

Index

Numerals in italics include an illustration of the subject mentioned.

A

Abercrombie, Ensign William W., 85, 91
Adams, Ensign John, 65
Africa (British battleship), 22, *23*, 25
Aichi dive bombers, *60-61*, 71, 127. *See also* Vals
Aiko, Captain Fumio, 44
"Airedales," *100-113*
Akagi (Japanese carrier), *cover*, 32, 37, 38, 39, 43, 44, *45*, 46, 47, 49, *50-59;* and Midway, 85, 89-90, 91, 93, 94, 96, 97
Aleutian Islands, *map* 62-63, 83, 84, 86, 97, 99
Amagi (Japanese carrier), 160
Argus (British carrier), *14-15*, 25, 28, 29, 30
Arizona (U.S. battleship), 47, 49
Aroostook (U.S. seaplane tender), 35
Arresting gear, 118-*119*
Astoria (U.S. cruiser), 96
Atlantic Ocean: U.S. Atlantic Fleet, 45; U.S. escort carriers in, *123-127*, 132
Australia, 61, *map* 62-63, 115, 117
Australia (British battle cruiser), *26*
Avengers (Grumman TBFs and TBMs), 85, 86, 89, *102-103, 144-145;* in Atlantic, 123, *124*, *126-127;* and U.S. offensive, 115, 117, 118, 134, 135, 137, 142, 155, 159

B

B-17, 85, 86, 90
B-25, 68
B-26, 85, 86, 89
B-29 Superfortress, 142, 159, 170
Bagdanovich, Commander M. P., quoted, 135
Bagley, Laurence, painting by, *42*
Barnes, Lieutenant William, quoted, 96
Battleships, 22, 27, 32; British, *27*, *29*; Japanese, 36-37, 39-40. *See also Yamato*
Beatty, Admiral Sir David, *24*, 25, 27, 29; quoted, 24
Bettys (Mitsubishi G4Ms), 65, 116, 164
Birmingham (U.S. cruiser), *6-7*, 21, 25
Bismarck Sea (U.S. escort carrier), 160
Blackburn reconnaissance plane, *14-15*
Bogue (U.S. escort carrier), *123-127*
Bougainville (Solomons), *map* 62-63, *map* 70, *map* 72, 131, 132, 134
Brett, Lieutenant Commander Jimmy, 69
Bristol Scout, *11*
British Admiralty, 11, 14, 22, 28; Air Department, 25. *See also* Royal Navy
British carriers, 7, *10-11*, *12-13*, *14-15*, *18*, *22-23*, 24-25, 27-29, *30*, 32, 41, *42*-43; versus Japan, 164, 166, 170
Browning, Captain Miles, 88
Buckmaster, Captain Elliott, 73, 96, 99
Buffalo planes, 85, 86
Bunker Hill (U.S. carrier), 134, 135, 149; and defeat of Japan, 164, *168*, 170
Buracker, Commander William H., quoted, 88
Buttlar-Brandenfels, Horst Treusch von, quoted, 28-29

C

Cabot (U.S. carrier), 157
California (U.S. battleship), 49
Campania (British seaplane carrier), 25
Caroline Islands, *map* 62-63, 139. *See also* Truk
Catapults, *118-119*
Cats (Catalina PBYs), 85, 86, 99, 122
Chambers, Captain Washington I., 21-22, 24, 31
Chance Vought planes. *See* Corsairs; Vindicators
Chitose (Japanese carrier), 135
Chiyoda (Japanese carrier), 142, 155
Clark, Vice Admiral Joseph J., quoted, 170
Coral Sea, *map* 62-63, 115; Battle of, 61, 68-75, *map* 70, *71*, *map* 72, *73*, *74-75*, 83, 84, 115, 133, 156
Corsairs (Chance Vought F4Us), 132, *148-149;* and defeat of Japan, 159, 160, 164, 166
Courageous (British carrier), 32
Craven, Captain Thomas T., 31, 32; quoted, 31
Curtiss, Glenn, 21
Curtiss planes, *6-7*, *8-9*, 21-22. *See also* Helldivers

D

Daly, Joseph, quoted, 116
Dauntlesses (Douglas SBDs), 62, 64, 65-66, 69, 70, 72, *78-79*, *100-101*, *104;* and Midway, 86, *87*, 88, 90, 93-97, *95;* and U.S. offensive, *114-115*, 117, 118, 122, 127-128, 134, 135, 142
De Chevalier, Lieutenant Commander Godfrey, 31-32
Devastators (Douglas TBDs), 62, 69, 72, *76-77*, 145; and Midway, 85, 88, *90*, 91-93
Dibb, Ensign Robert, quoted, 95
Dickinson, Lieutenant Clarence, quoted, 64
Dive bombers, *cover*, *60-61*, 62, 69, 71, *86-87*, 93, *106*. *See also* Dauntlesses; Helldivers; Vals; Vindicators
Dixon, Lieutenant Commander Robert E., 69, 70
Dogfights, 117, 128, 140
Dönitz, Admiral Karl, quoted, 123
Doolittle, Lieutenant Colonel James H., 68
Douglas planes. *See* Dauntlesses; Devastators
Dunning, Squadron Commander E. H., 28
Dutch Harbor (Aleutians), *map* 62-63, 86

E

Eagle (British carrier), 29
Earnest, Ensign Bert, 89; quoted, 89
Ely, Eugene, *6-7*, *8-9*, *20-21*, 21-22, 24, 25, 29; quoted, 24
Emerson, A. C., *128*
Engadine (British seaplane carrier), 24, *25*
Eniwetok (Marshalls), *map* 62-63, 136-138
Enterprise (U.S. carrier), *cover*, 44, 45; and Coral Sea, 61, 64-65, 68; and Midway, 83-85, 88, 91-94, 97, 99; and U.S. offensive, 115, 118, 120, 121, 122, 127, 128, 130-131, 133, 159, 164
Escort carriers (CVEs), 132, *143;* in Atlantic, *123-127;* and defeat of Japan, 159-160, 166; and Philippines, *150-151*, *154*, 155-156, 157
Essex (U.S. carrier), 134, 135, 157, 166
Essex-class carriers, 132, *137*. *See also Lexington* (1943)
Ewing, Harvey, quoted, 169

F

Fanshaw Bay (U.S. escort carrier), 151
Farragut (U.S. destroyer), 121
Ferrier, Harry, quoted, 89
Fieberling, Lieutenant Langdon K., 85, 86, 89
Flatley, Lieutenant Commander James "Jimmy," 71-72, 84, 127
Fletcher, Admiral Frank Jack: and Coral Sea, 65, 68, 69, 70, 72, 75; and Midway, 85, 86, 88, 96; and U.S. offensive, 115, 117-118, 120
Flight-deck operations, *100-113*
Flying boats: Japanese, 65, 66, 69, 85. *See also* Cats; Seaplanes
Fowler, B. F., *11*
Franklin (U.S. carrier), *162-163*, 163-164
Fuchida, Commander Mitsuo, 85, 93, 94, 96; quoted, 45, 46-47, 93, 94
Fukudome, Rear Admiral Shigeru, 41; quoted, 40
Furious (British cruiser), *12-13*, 14, 28-29, *30*

G

Gaido, Bruno P., 65, 94, 99
Gambier Bay (U.S. escort carrier), 155-156
Garlow, Clarence, 127
Gary, Lieutenant Donald, quoted, 164
Gay, Ensign George "Tex," *82-83;* quoted, 88, *90*, *91*-92, 99
Gayler, Lieutenant Noel, quoted, 73
Gehres, Captain Leslie H., quoted, 164
Genda, Lieutenant Commander Minoru, *37*, 41, 43, 44; and Midway, 85-86, 88, 91, 96; quoted, 37, 43, 44
Gilbert Islands, *map* 62-63, 133, 136
Glorious (British carrier), 32
Grumman planes, 161. *See also* Avengers; Hellcats; Wildcats
Guadalcanal (Solomons), *map* 62-63, *map* 70, *map* 72, *121*, 133, 134; Henderson Field, 116, 120-121, 122, 130-132; Naval Battle of, 131; and U.S. offensive, 115-118, 120-122, 130-132
Guam (Marianas), *map* 62-63, 139, 140

H

Hackleback (U.S. submarine), 166
Halsey, Admiral William F., Jr., 64, 84, *159;* and Philippines, 152, 157-158, 159; and U.S. offensive, 122, 133-134
Hamilton, Lieutenant Commander W. L., quoted, 69, 70
Hammann (U.S. destroyer), 99
Hampton Roads, Va., *6-7*, 21
Hancock (U.S. carrier), 166
Hellcats (Grumman F6Fs), *100-101*, *102*, *106-107*, *110*, 145, *148-149;* and defeat of Japan, 160-161, *164*, 166; and Philippines, *154*, 156, 159; and U.S. offensive, 132, *133*, 134, 135, 137, 140-141, 142
Helldivers (Curtiss SB2Cs), *112-113*, 132, 135, 137, 142, *146-147*, 155, 159, 166-167
Hermes (British carrier), *18*, 29
Hirohito, Emperor, 152
Hiroshima, Japan, *map* 62-63, 170
Hiryu (Japanese carrier), 85, 96, 97
Hiyo (Japanese carrier), 122, 142
Holmberg, Lieutenant Paul, 95
Holt, William "Wild Bill," 116
Homes, Lieutenant Commander Gerard, 25
Hornet (U.S. carrier, 1941), 44, 45, 61, 68; and Midway, *82-83*, 84-85, 86, 88, 91, 96, 99; and U.S. offensive, 115, 121, 122, 127, *128*, *129*, 130
Hornet (U.S. carrier, 1943), 132, *161*
Hosho (Japanese carrier), *18*, 37, 39, 43, 62
Hughes, Charles Evans, 32
Hydroaeroplanes, 11

I

Illustrious (British carrier), *42*-43, 166
Indefatigable (British carrier), 24, 166, 170
Independence (U.S. carrier), 134, 159
Independence-class carriers, 132
Indomitable (British carrier), 166
Inoguchi, Captain Rikihei, quoted, 156
Inoue, Admiral Shigeyoshi, 75
Intelligence, 68, 84, 85, 99, *130*, 132, 140. *See also* Radar; Reconnaissance
Intrepid (U.S. carrier), 138, 157, 170

Irvine, Ensign Charles B., 127
Itaya, Commander Shigeru, 45, 47
Iwo Jima, *map* 62-63, 159, 160

J

Japanese Army, 37-38, 40, 61, 68, 122; and *kikusui* campaign, 166-167, 169-170
Japanese carriers, *cover,* 7, 22, 24, 29; and Coral Sea, 61-75; early, 7, *18,* 36-38, *39-40, 41;* and Midway, 83-99; and Pearl Harbor, 38-41, 43-47, *45,* 49, *50-59;* and Philippines, 152-159; and U.S. offensive, 115-142
Japanese Marines, 61, 122
Japanese Naval Air Service, 36-37
Japanese Navy: Combined Fleet, 36-37, 39, 43, 139, 152; and *kikusui* campaign, 166-167, 169-170; and naval limitation treaties, 32, 34, 37, 39, 44; pilots, *41. See also* Japanese carriers; Kamikazes
Jills (Nakajima Tenzan), *144-145*
Judys (Yokosuka D4Y Suisei), 141, *146-147,* 155
Junyo (Japanese carrier), 86, 97; and U.S. offensive, 122, 128, 142
Jupiter (U.S. carrier), 31
Jurika, Lieutenant Commander Stephen, Jr., 163
Jutland, Battle of, 24, *25,* 151

K

Kaga (Japanese carrier), 32, 37, 38, 39, *40, 41,* 44, 47, *52-53;* and Midway, 85, *90,* 91, 92, 93-94, 97
Kagoshima Bay, Japan, 44
Kamikazes, 147, 160, 164, 166-167, 169-170; and Philippines, *150, 152,* 156-159. *See also* Zeros, and kamikazes
Kanno, Flight Warrant Officer Kenzo, 72
Kates (Nakajima B5Ns), 45, 46, *57,* 71, 73, *76-77,* 97, 128, 145
Kawanishi planes: H8K flying boats, 85; George, 160-161. *See also* Mavis
Kikusui campaign (kamikazes), 166-167, 169-170
King, Admiral Ernest J., 64, *67,* 142
Kinkaid, Rear Admiral Thomas C., 122, 127
Kiska Island, *map* 62-63, 99
Kitkun Bay (U.S. escort carrier), *143,* 151
Knox, Frank, *67*
Kobayashi, Lieutenant Michio, 96
Koga, Admiral Mineichi, 134, 137-138
Kure, Japan, *39, map* 62-63, 160, 163
Kurile Islands, *map* 62-63; Hitokappu Bay, 44, *50-51*
Kusaka, Rear Admiral Ryunosuke, 43, 44
Kwajalein (Marshalls), *map* 62-63, 64, *136*
Kyushu, Japan, *map* 62-63, 159, 160, 166

L

Lae, New Guinea, *map* 62-63, 67, 131
Langley (U.S. carrier), *16-17,* 31-35, *33, 34*
Lansdowne (U.S. destroyer), 121
Lea, Tom, painting by, *128*
Lentz, Seaman Herbert, quoted, 75
Leslie, Max, 93-97
Lexington (U.S. carrier, 1927), 32, 33-35, *34,* 44, 45, 117, 133; and Coral Sea, 61, 64, 65-75, *map* 70, *map* 72, *73, 74-75*
Lexington (U.S. carrier, 1943), 132, *133, 137, 140,* 141, 155
Leyte (Philippines), *map* 62-63, 151-152, 157, 158
Leyte Gulf (Philippines), *map* 62-63; Battle of, 151-153, *154,* 155-156, 160, 166
Life (magazine), photographs by, *92-95*
Lightnings (Lockheed P-38s), 132
Lindsey, Lieutenant Commander Eugene, 88, 92
Luzon (Philippines), *map* 62-63, 151, 155, 157, 159

M

MacArthur, General Douglas, 142, 152, 156-159
McCampbell, David, quoted, 149
McClusky, Lieutenant Commander Clarence Wade, 88, 94, 95; quoted, 93
McCuskey, Ensign Scotty, 65; quoted, 65
McKenna, Captain F. J., 151
Majuro (Marshalls), *map* 62-63, 136, 139-140
Makigumo (Japanese destroyer), 99
Makin (Gilberts), *map* 62-63, 65, 136
Malaya, 43, 49, 61, *map* 62-63
Manchuria, 37-38, 40, *map* 62-63
Manila (Philippines), *map* 62-63, 157, *158*
Manila Bay (Philippines), *153*
Manning, Jay, quoted, 89
Manxman (British seaplane carrier), 25, 27
Marcus Island, *map* 62-63, *130*
Mariana Islands, *map* 62-63, 139-140, 142, 156, 159, 170; Turkey Shoot, 142, 152. *See also* Guam; Saipan
Marshall Islands, *map* 62-63, 64, 65, *134-135,* 136-140
Maryland (U.S. battleship), 166
Massey, Lieutenant Commander Lance, 86, 92-93
Mavis (Kawanishi H6K), 65, 66
Mears, Lieutenant Fred, quoted, 115
Mexican Revolution, 30
Midway Island, 45, *map* 62-63; Battle of, *cover,* 78, 83-99, 115, 118, 122, 127, 132, 136
Mikawa, Vice Admiral Gunichi, 117
Mikuma (Japanese cruiser), 97
Mindoro (Philippines), *map* 62-63, 158-159
Mississippi (U.S. battleship), 32
Mitchell, General William "Billy," 30-31
Mitscher, Vice Admiral Marc: and defeat of Japan, 160, 163, 164, 166, 169-170; and Philippines, 153, 155, 157; quoted, 170; and U.S. offensive, 136-142, *140*
Mitsubishi planes. *See* Bettys; Zeros
Moffett, Rear Admiral William A., 32, *33,* 37
Mogami (Japanese cruiser), *95,* 97
Montgomery, Rear Admiral Alfred E., 134, 135
Moore, Lieutenant Raymond A., 91; quoted, 88
Mori, Chief Flight Petty Officer Juzo, quoted, 47
Morrow, Dwight W., and Morrow Board, 33
Murata, Lieutenant Commander Shigeharu, 46, 127, 128
Murray, Captain George, 65

N

Nagara (Japanese cruiser), 96
Nagasaki, Japan, *map* 62-63, 170
Nagato (Japanese battleship), *36*
Nagumo, Admiral Chuichi, 43, 44, *45,* 49; and Midway, 85-86, 88-91, 92, 93, 96; quoted, 45; and U.S. offensive, 122, 127, 128, 139
Nakajima planes, 71, 127. *See also* Jills; Kates
Naval arms limitations 32, 39, 44; Washington Naval Conference, 32, 34, 37, 39
Neosho (U.S. oiler), 69, *map* 70, 71, 75
Netherlands East Indies, 43, 49, 61, *map* 62-63, 158
Nevada (U.S. battleship), 49
New Georgia (Solomons), *map* 62-63, 131, 134
New Guinea, 61, *map* 62-63, 67, 68, *map* 70, *map* 72; and U.S. offensive, 131-132, 137, 142. *See also* Port Moresby
New Jersey (U.S. battleship), 159
Nimitz, Admiral Chester W., 68; and Midway, 83, 84, *85,* 91; quoted, 142; and U.S. offensive, 115, 133, 134, 142
Nishizawa, Warrant Officer Hiroyoshi, 114

O

O'Callahan, Father Joseph T., 164; quoted, 163
O'Flaherty, Ensign Frank W., 94, 99
O'Hare, Lieutenant Edward "Butch," 66, *67*
Ohka (Cherry Blossom) bombs, 164, 166
Okinawa, *map* 62-63, 159, 160, 164, 166-*167,* 169-170
Oklahoma (U.S. battleship), 49
Onishi, Admiral Takijiro, 41, 43, 44, 156-157
Ostfriesland (German battleship), 32
Oyodo (Japanese cruiser), 155
Ozawa, Admiral Jisaburo, 139, 140-142; and Philippines, 152-153, 155-156

P

Pacific Ocean, *map* 62-63
Panama Canal, 99, 157; U.S. Navy war games at, 33, 34-35, 37
Panay (U.S. gunboat), 38
Patterson (U.S. destroyer), 117
Pearl Harbor, Hawaii, 38-41, 43-47, *48-49,* 51, *58-59, map* 62-63, 121, 127, 136, 153, 156; and Coral Sea, 61, *64,* 68, 75, 78; Ford Island, *46,* 47, 49; and Midway, 83, 84, 85, *91,* 99
Pennsylvania (U.S. cruiser), *8-9, 20-21,* 22, 24
Phelps (U.S. destroyer), 75
Philippines, 38, 43, 61, *map* 62-63; U.S. reconquest of, 142, 151-159. *See also* Leyte Gulf
Philippine Sea, *map* 62-63; Battle of the, *140-*142, 145, 155
Pittsburgh (U.S. cruiser), 163
Pontoons, *10,* 11, 24-25. *See also* Seaplanes
Port Moresby, New Guinea, *map* 62-62, 68, 75, 83, 132
Powers, Lieutenant John J., 72
Pownall, Rear Admiral C. A., 136
Pratt, Admiral William V., 35-36; quoted, 35
Pride, Lieutenant Alfred M., 32
Princeton (U.S. carrier), *131,* 133, 148, 155
Puget Sound Navy Yard (Washington), *34*

Q

Queen Mary (British battle cruiser), 24

R

Rabaul, New Britain, *60-61, map* 62-63, 65-67, 75; and U.S. offensive, 115-117, 121, *131-*135, 151, 159, 163
Radar, 62, 66, 86, 96, 97; and defeat of Japan, 151, 159, 163; and U.S. offensive, 118, 121, 132, 140. *See also* Intelligence
Ramsey, Captain Dewitt, 121
Ramsey, Lieutenant Commander Paul, 70, 71, 72
Ranger (U.S. carrier), 18, *19*
Reconnaissance, 69, 85, 97; and U.S. offensive, 118, 130, 136, 140. *See also* Intelligence; Radar
Reeves, Captain Joseph M., *33*
Rheims, France, air show, 7
Roosevelt, Franklin D., 38, 43, *67*
Royal Air Force, 29, 65
Royal Flying Corps, 22
Royal Naval Air Service, 24, 29, 36
Royal Navy, 7, 11, 14, 25, 27-29, 43; Battle Cruiser Fleet, 24; and naval limitation treaties, 32, 34, 37, 39, 44
Runyon, Ensign Donald, 118

Russo-Japanese War, 36, 37
Rutland, Flight Lieutenant Frederick J., 24, *25,* 27, 28
Ryujo (Japanese carrier), 39, 62; and Midway, 86, 97; and U.S. offensive, 118

S

St. Lo (U.S. escort carrier), 151, 155
Saipan (Marianas), *map* 62-63, 139-140, *141,* 142
Sakai, Flight Petty Officer Saburo, *116*-117; quoted, 116, 161
Salamaua, New Guinea, *map* 62-63, 67, 131
Samson, Lieutenant Charles Rumney, *22-23,* 25
San Diego, Calif., 33, 38, 44, 99, 136; North Island Naval Air Station, 64
San Francisco, Calif.: Bay, *8-9,* 22, *170-171; Examiner,* 22
Sangamon (U.S. escort carrier), *150*
Santa Cruz Islands, *map* 62-63, 122; Battle of the, 128, *129,* 130
Saratoga (U.S. carrier), 32, 33-36, *34,* 37, 44, 62, 64, 99; and U.S. offensive, 115, 116, 118, 121, 130, *131,* 133, 160
Seaplane carriers, 24, *25,* 27
Seaplanes, 7, *10-11, 12-13,* 24-25, 27, 28, 30, 37, 116; folding-wing, *22. See also* Pontoons; Seaplane carriers
Seki, Lieutenant Commander Manoru, 127; quoted, 127
Sherman, Rear Admiral Frederick C. "Ted," 66, 75, 133-134, 135
Shiga, Lieutenant Yoshio, 47, 49
Shimazaki, Lieutenant Commander Shizekazu, 46, 49; quoted, 75
Shoho (Japanese carrier), 62, 68, *map* 70, *71,* 75
Shokaku (Japanese carrier), 46, 39, 83, 99; and Coral Sea, 68, 69, *map* 70, 72-73, *map* 73, 75; and U.S. offensive, 118, 121, 127, 128, 142
Short planes, 28; S.38, 22, *23;* Sunbeam seaplane, 24
Sims (U.S. destroyer), 69, *map* 70, 71, 75
Smart, Flight Sublieutenant B. A., 27
Smith, R. C., painting by, *cover*
Solomon Islands, *map* 62-63, 68; Battle of the Eastern Solomons, 115-118, 120-122; and U.S. offensive, 115-118, 120-122, 131-134. *See also* Bougainville; Guadalcanal; Tulagi
Sopwith planes, *13, 14, 26;* Camel, *26,* 28-29, *30;* Cuckoo torpedo, 29; Pup, *10-11, 12,* 27, 28
Soryu (Japanese carrier), *39,* 47, *94;* and Midway, 85, 92-95, 97
South Dakota (U.S. battleship), 140
Spruance, Rear Admiral Raymond A.: and Midway, 84, 85, 86, 88-89, 97; and U.S. offensive, 136-137, 139, 140, 142, 159
Stetson, Lieutenant Thomas, 169
Strong, Lieutenant Stockton B., 127
Submarines: German (U-boats), *123-127,* 132; Japanese, 85, 99, 121, 142; U.S., 85, 140, 142, 156, 166, 170
Sueter, Captain Murray, 25
Sugita, Naval Aviation Pilot Shoishi, 160-161
Suwannee (U.S. escort carrier), *154*
Swordfish (Fairey), *42-43*

T

Taiho (Japanese carrier), 142
Takagi, Admiral Takeo, 68, 69, 71, 72, 75
Takahashi, Lieutenant Commander Kakuichi, 46; and Coral Sea, 69, 71, 72
Taranto, Italy, 41, *42-43*
Tarawa (Gilberts), *map* 62-63, 133, 136
Tennessee (U.S. battleship), *48-49*
Thach, Lieutenant Commander John S. "Jimmy," 62, *64,* 66, 157-158; and Midway, 84, 92, 93, 95, 96; quoted, 64, 66, 67, 95, 158. *See also* "Thach weave"
"Thach weave," *64-65,* 69, 73, 95-96, 116, 135, 157-158
Threadfin (U.S. submarine), 166
Ticonderoga (U.S. carrier), 159, *164*
Tiny Tim rockets, 160, 164
Tojo, General Hideki, 131
Tokyo, Japan, *map* 62-63, 160, 170
Tokyo Express, 121, 131. *See also* Guadalcanal
Tondern, Germany, 28-29, *31*
Tone (Japanese cruiser), 88, 90
Torpedo planes, *51,* 62, 69, 70, 71; and Midway, 84-85, 86, 89-91, 93. *See also* Avengers; Devastators; Jills; Kates
Truk (Carolines), *map* 62-63, 122, 134-*138,* 140, 157
Tulagi (Solomons), *map* 62-63, 68, *map* 70, *map* 72, 75; and U.S. offensive, 115, 116

U

Ulithi, *map* 62-63, 157, 164
U.S. Army, 31, 132, 152, 169; Air Forces, 65
U.S. carriers, *cover,* 22, 24, 43; and Coral Sea, 61-75; early, *6-7, 8-9, 16-17,* 18, *19,* 21-22, 29-36, *33, 34;* and Midway, 83-99; and Philippines, 142, 152-159; and U.S. offensive, 115-142. *See also* Escort carriers
U.S. Marine Corps, 45, 47, 49, 85, 86, 90; and defeat of Japan, 152, 159, 160; and U.S. offensive, 115, 116, 121, 130-131, 141
U.S. Navy, 24, 29, 30-35; Atlantic Fleet, 45; Bureau of Aeronautics, 32; Fast Carrier Task Force, 136, 139; and early carriers, 7, 17, 21-22; Fifth Fleet, 135-142; and naval limitation treaties, 32, 34, 37, 39, 44; South Pacific Forces, 122; Third Fleet, 152. *See also* U.S. carriers; U.S. Pacific Fleet
U.S. Pacific Fleet, 61, 62, 83, 99, 115, 153; and Pearl Harbor, 38-41, 43-47, *46,* 49. *See also* U.S. carriers; U.S. Navy

V

Valencia, Lieutenant Eugene A., quoted, 137
Vals (Aichi D3As), 46, 96; and Coral Sea, 71, 73, 75, *78-79;* and U.S. offensive, 118, 120, 128
Vejtasa, Lieutenant Stanley W., 128
Victorious (British carrier), 166
Vindex (British carrier), *10-11*
Vindicators (Chance Vought SB2Us), 85, 86, 90, 91
Vose, Lieutenant Commander James E. "Moe," 128, 135
Vought planes, 16-17
Vraciu, Lieutenant Alexander, 140-141

W

Wake Island, 45, 61, *map* 62-63, *114-115*
Waldron, Commander John C., 84-85, 86, 91; quoted, 86
Washington Naval Conference. *See* Naval arms limitations
Wasp (U.S. carrier, 1940), 99, 115, 118, *121,* 132
Wasp (U.S. carrier, 1943), 163, 164
Watson, Ernest, quoted, 27
West Virginia (U.S. battleship), *48-49*
White Plains (U.S. escort carrier), 151
Whiting, Commander Kenneth, 31-33; quoted, 33
Widhelm, Lieutenant Commander William J. "Gus," 127-128; quoted, 127, 128
Wildcats (Grumman F4Fs), 62, 64-67, 69, 70, 71, 73, *80-81, 110;* in Atlantic, *123, 124;* and Midway, 84-88, 92, *93,* 95-97; and "Thach weave," 64-*65;* and U.S. offensive, 116-117, 118, 127-*128*
World War I, 7, *10-11,* 13, 22, 24-*25,* 27-29, 30; Armistice, 29; Japan and, 37, 38. *See also* Zeppelins
World War II, 7, 22, 24. *See also* Coral Sea; Midway; Pearl Harbor; Philippines; U.S. carriers

Y

Yahagi (Japanese cruiser), 166, 169
Yamaguchi, Rear Admiral Tamon, 96, 97
Yamamoto, Admiral Isoroku, *36,* 37, 39, 40, 43-44, 68; and Midway, 83-84, 85, 97, 99; quoted, 41, 61, 97; and U.S. offensive, 118, 120, 122, 131-132, 134
Yamato (Japanese battleship), 83, 85, 91, 97; and defeat of Japan, 160, 166-*167,* 169
Yap (Carolines), *map* 62-63, 139
Yarmouth (British carrier), 27, 28
Yokosuka planes. *See* Judys
Yorktown (U.S. carrier, 1937), 44, 45; and Coral Sea, 61, 64, 65, 68, 69-75, *map* 70, *map* 72; and Midway, 84-86, 88, 91-97, *98-99;* and U.S. offensive, 117, *118, 130, 138*
Yorktown (U.S. carrier, 1943), 132, 169, *170-171*
Yoshida, Ensign Mitsuru, quoted, 167, 169

Z

Zeppelins, 25; *L 23,* 27-29; at Tondern, Germany, 28-29, *31*
Zeros (Mitsubishi A6Ms), 45-47, 49, 50, *54-55, 56-57,* 62, 64; and Coral Sea, 69-73, *80-81;* and kamikazes, 151, *153, 154,* 156-157; and Midway, 89-97, *94;* and "Thach weave," 64-*65;* and U.S. offensive, 116-117, 118, 122, 127-128, 134-135, 137
Zuiho (Japanese carrier), 62, 122, 127, 155
Zuikaku (Japanese carrier), 39, *52-53,* 83, 99; and Coral Sea, 68, *map* 70, *map* 72, 73, 75; and U.S. offensive, 118, 121, 128, 142